BACK TO THE BASEX

BACK TO THE BASEX

A RECLAMATION OF SEX ENERGY FOR MEN

BORIS CHESTNUT

Published by
Continuum Operations LLC
www.backtothebasex.com

Book Design and Formatting by
Brand It Beautifully™
www.branditbeautifully.com

Author Photography by
Chelse Lilly
www.takenbystorm.co

ISBN for Paperback version: 979-8-9926041-0-8
ISBN for Hardcover version: 979-8-9926041-1-5
ISBN for Digital version: 979-8-9926041-2-2

Printed in the United States of America

DEDICATION

"To my mother, the epitome of divine feminine energy, whose love has been a guiding light throughout my life. From my earliest days, you have shown me what it means to express healthy love and connection. You taught me the importance of compassion and resilience, nurturing my spirit while also holding me accountable. You had a unique way of calling me out when I was wrong—doing so with grace and love—ensuring that I learned valuable lessons without ever feeling belittled in public. Your unwavering support has been my anchor through both the storms and the calm of life. You have stood firm by my side in every situation, providing a safe haven where I could grow and flourish. Your strength and wisdom have shaped my understanding of love, and I am forever grateful to have you as my mother, my best friend, and my greatest inspiration.

"To my father, the steadfast protector of our family, who worked tirelessly to provide us with a life filled with security and opportunity. Your dedication to ensuring that we never had to worry about food, clothing, or summer vacations speaks volumes about your love and commitment to our family. You have shown me the essence of the American dream, and your perseverance in the face of challenges as a Black family has instilled in me a deep appreciation for hard work and determination. While our relationship has had its share of ups and downs, I cherish the moments we've shared in both joy and conflict. Those moments of disagreement have often led to the most meaningful

conversations, teaching me the power of forgiveness and understanding. I appreciate the fights we've had, for they have ultimately brought us closer together, reinforcing the unconditional love that binds us as father and son.

"And to my sister, my confidante and unwavering supporter, I am profoundly grateful for the bond we share. Even though we don't always see eye to eye on various matters, our differences have only strengthened my appreciation for your perspective and character. You have been my rock, standing by me through thick and thin, and I am grateful for the love and loyalty you consistently show. I remember asking God for a sister before you were born, and having you in my life has been one of the greatest blessings I could have ever wished for. Together, we have navigated the complexities of family and life, and I treasure the unique connection we share, built on mutual respect and understanding.

"This book is as much a dedication to you as it is a testament to the love, support, and guidance that each of you has provided me throughout my life. It reflects the lessons learned from our shared experiences and the values instilled in me by our family. May it inspire others to cherish and honor the relationships that have shaped them, just as I have been shaped by yours. To my family—thank you for being my foundation, my motivation, and my greatest blessings."

TABLE OF CONTENTS

SPIRITUAL FOREWORD

Each book on the shelf makes a promise to the person who buys it—that it will uplift, enlighten, and entertain them. The reader is often disappointed. I can say, in this case, Boris Chestnut delivers the goods. What a wonderful read! Mr. Chestnut is highly educated and accomplished, but when he talks to people, he is down-to-earth and almost humble. He writes that way too. Reading his book feels like talking to a regular guy—except what he is saying is exceptional wisdom.

In this book, he shares his insights about sex, particularly examining sexuality through a spiritual lens. It's an old topic to which he brings a fresh perspective. You can tell he has helped his clients, but more importantly, he has truly listened to them. His insights reflect the kind of understanding that comes from listening with the heart, not just going through the motions.

I have taught thousands of students and trained hundreds of life coaches and professionals. So when I tell you this book can help you on your journey, you should listen to me. He tackles familiar topics like erectile dysfunction and offers new and exciting perspectives on them. He also speaks about preventing the leakage of sexual energy in men—a subject near and dear to my heart. He writes from an experience set that few men can match. You will enjoy the section on his concept of "pussy prayer." I won't spoil it for you (LOL), but it's my favorite part of the book.

My goal in my practice is to assist my clients in becoming the highest and best versions of themselves. I believe Boris Chestnut shares that same goal. It starts with the discovery of a man's self-identity. How does a man uncover his true, natal self? The answers are scattered throughout this book. I think what Mr. Chestnut has done is construct a tool for inner discovery. As a man reads each chapter, he embarks on a journey of self-exploration, gradually building a library of insights about himself. This book can serve as a guide to help men reach their highest and best selves.

We should note for the record that male potency has declined over the past 40 years. At the same time, men are experiencing more sexual issues than at any point in history. Even if a man enjoys good health and dedicates time to the gym, he is still exposed to stress and negativity. In fact, most causes of lost sexual power today are psychological rather than physical. Not the least of these influences is feminism itself. *Back to the Basex* is a gift to modern men—a roadmap to reclaiming their optimal prime. We can thank Boris Chestnut for putting in the effort to write such a book. It is truly a tool for men to reclaim their sexual energy. I highly recommend this book. Climb inside yourself and discover what's really there!

Master Yao Nyamekye
Founder of the Grand Trine Organization

FOREWORD

When I met Greg Dawson several years ago through a mutual friend, I was intrigued. In the field of sexology, there are only a few Black male professionals, so the opportunity to meet another brother meant a lot to me. Over time, we quickly learned about each other's experiences in the field, and it has always felt like he understood, empathized, and remained insightful about being Black in a predominantly white profession.

When Greg asked me to offer a foreword to his book, *Back to BaSex*, I was honored and flattered. Greg spoke of writing a book for years, and I'm happy that it has come to fruition. Over the years, Dawson has spoken charismatically about illuminating the sexual and spiritual experiences of Black folks and their relationships. His book is meticulous in its description and analysis of friendships, romantic relationships, and the relationship that a person may have with oneself. He offers several opportunities for the reader to critique self-care and then determine how the love of oneself becomes integrated into the expectations that one might have in romantic partnerships.

What's compelling about Greg's book is that it gives the reader an opportunity to reflect upon the erotic potential and sexual response of Black men. Dawson's book is cutting-edge in that he offers professional and personal accounts of men navigating their emotional, sexual, and spiritual experiences, making this book a must-read for all. Greg is, by far, one of the most talented professionals I know, offering truth and light to practice and love.

Dawson's understanding and application of the precepts of Tantra allow for a different perspective on the intersection and impact of incorporating healing energy into sexuality. Moreover, his extensive experience using mindfulness techniques to help people become grounded and centered offers a "breath of fresh air" in assisting men and their partners to become more actualized and grounded in their sexual relationships. Finally, Dawson includes chapters on the use of mushrooms and cannabis for readers to consider the possibility of enhancing sexual response and expression.

Greg Dawson's book is a celebration of sexuality in the past, present, and future. It is an essential read for practitioners who clinically engage with Black men. It is also a book that empowers lay readers to feel a greater sense of connection to the Black men they seek love or partnership with.

James C. Wadley, Ph.D
Editor-in-Chief
Journal of Black Sexuality and Relationships

INTRODUCTION

Namaste. It's only right to begin this book with a prayer to intentionally honor the energy of women. Through what I've been taught in tantric spaces and what I believe, I've come to know that it is essential to honor and worship women and their divine feminine energy. It's my hope that, as men, you use this technique to manage yourself, heal, transmute, and create the life you so desire.

THE PUSSY PRAYER

In the dim glow of the moonlit room, Ethan sat cross-legged, his eyes closed, focusing on his breath. Beside him, Lily lay enveloped in the soft embrace of the sheets, her presence a calming balm to his restless spirit. Tonight was about healing, release, and the sacred connection they shared.

It was time. Lily shifted herself from her position in bed and sat on top of her man, wrapping her legs firmly around his waist with the bottom of her feet connecting perfectly. Ethan maintained a firm 90-degree angle. He suddenly felt tension coming to an ease. He'd been anticipating this moment all throughout his hard day at work, and he remembered the text messages from Lily telling him about how she needed him to rest his mind. Ethan's consciousness was still firmly in his mind, busy thinking about the worries of the world. Ethan became firmly erect due to the soft touch and scent Lily gifted him. He loved rose oil. He also knew that when she wore rose oil, she meant business.

Ethan was now inside. His eyes closed even tighter as he thought about his pains and woes. Shifting his conscious energy, he visualized a stream of light moving from his mind and down through his body. This light carried with it the burdens he had been holding on to—his struggles, pains, and troubles, all swirling in a vortex of emotion. As he shifted his focus to his core, the energy transformed, merging with his deepest desires and intentions.

In the quiet sanctuary of their shared space, Ethan leaned forward, his forehead resting gently against Lily's abdomen. Eyes closed, he whispered a heartfelt prayer, a soft incantation of gratitude to the sacred space they shared.

"Thank you," he murmured, voice barely above a whisper, "for being my refuge, my safe haven. In you, I find release from the chaos of the world, a place where I am seen and understood."

His hands rested on her hips, feeling the warmth and energy radiating between them.

"Every day, I carry the weight of stress and misunderstanding, but here, with you, I find peace. You are my sanctuary, and in this sacred union, I am free to let go."

As their energies intertwined, they became a perfect symbol of masculine and feminine energy. He was the grounding masculine for the feminine, creating healing through pleasure. Ethan visualized a wave of calm washing over them, cleansing and renewing them both.

He uttered softly in her ear, "Together, we create a space for healing and manifesting the understanding and prosperity we both seek."

With every breath, he felt the warmth of Lily's hand grounding him. She was his sanctuary, his haven where his vulnerability could be laid bare. As they connected, skin to skin, Ethan imagined the light flowing out from him and into her, a gentle, radiant stream. He visualized each worry dissolving, canceled out by the polarity of their energies.

In this intimate dance, the room became a cocoon of healing and renewal. The boundaries of their individual selves blurred, creating a space where mood and spirit could harmonize. It was here, in this sacred union, that Ethan sowed the seeds of prosperity.

Lily felt the shift, the warmth spreading through her in a serene yet powerful exchange. Together, they created a sanctuary of trust and transformation, their prayer unspoken yet deeply understood. Here, they manifested not only pleasure but a shared vision of abundance and peace.

As I delved deeper into these conversations, I realized that the silence surrounding male sexuality comes with profound consequences. Men often feel trapped in a cycle of expectation, where vulnerability is seen as a weakness and emotional expression is stifled. This creates a barrier to not only personal growth but also the richness of intimate relationships.

-Using this technique, you'll need high body awareness. During sex, when you feel the emissions process taking place specifically at the bottom of your tailbone, think intentionally about the answers you want and need. You can also consider the ways you want to manifest this new space and world you vehemently want to create. Focus your consciousness, from your mind to your body and the tip of the lingam, while intentionally sharing this energy with your partner(s).

WHY DID I CREATE THIS BOOK?

In my journey through behavioral health, sexual health, and tantric spaces, I have encountered men from various backgrounds carrying their own stories, struggles, and unspoken truths. Some revealed insecurities about performance, while others shared their longing for a deeper connection beyond the physical. These discussions illuminated a stark reality: Many of us are navigating our sexual lives in isolation, armed only with societal myths and outdated, ineffective ideals.

This book aims to break down those barriers, inviting men to engage in an open, honest dialogue about their experiences. We will explore what it means to be a sexual being in today's world, addressing the need for an education that goes beyond technique and delves into emotional intelligence and spiritual spaces meshed with pleasure.

Additionally, we will examine the intersection of sexuality and spirituality, recognizing that our intimate lives can be a sacred space for growth and healing. By fostering a deeper understanding of ourselves and our partner(s), we can transform our approach to intimacy from mere performance to a holistic experience that honors our bodies, emotions, and souls.

Ultimately, this journey is about reclaiming our narratives as men, raising our sex energy, and using it to fuel the lives we want and need. It's about learning to embrace our imperfections, celebrate our successes, and find joy in the journey of discovery. Together, let's create a culture where conversations about sex are not only welcomed but encouraged—a culture that values connection over conquest and intimacy over isolation. Let this be the beginning of a new dialogue where we can all learn, heal, and thrive as sexual beings.

Do all of this by having basic conversations with the energy of keeping it simple. Keep it basic—for now.

WHO IS THIS BOOK FOR?

I'm writing this book for men; for those of us who have struggled in silence, grappling with heartache, loss, and the looming shadow of our own expectations. One of the most profound experiences of my life unfolded during a breakup. This was a time when I found myself on the precipice of losing everything: my possessions, my financial stability, and my peace of mind. It was in this darkness that I truly discovered my character and the essence of the man I wanted to be.

Through the process of healing, I engaged in shadow work with my Tantra tribe, a supportive community that illuminated the path ahead. Together, we established a code—an agreement to honor ourselves and our energy. The challenge was immense: We were tasked with halting the leakage of our vital sexual energy, preserving it, and raising it to be used for good. This energy, when harnessed, became not only a source of prosperity but also a conduit for blessings that flowed both ways.

The benefits of this ritual were immediate and transformative. I began to honor myself and those around me in ways I had never imagined. Yet, I faltered at times. There were moments when I didn't uphold the code. I found myself using sexual encounters as mere transactions, treating partners as tools rather than the sacred beings they truly are. I neglected the deeper connection that could exist, and in doing so, I missed opportunities for genuine intimacy and growth.

This book is a call to action for men who have faced their own trials and tribulations—who have felt lost or disconnected, who have yearned for something more meaningful. It's for those who recognize the need to heal and create better, not just for themselves but for the world around them.

This isn't a guide to becoming the 'perfect' man or a manual of purity. Instead, it's a sanctuary for the imperfect—a place where we can acknowledge our flaws and still strive for greatness.

The aim is to help men establish a code that elevates us from Sahu (our base, primal selves) to Ab (our higher, enlightened selves). This journey is about reclaiming our sexual energy and using it as a force for good. It's also a testament to the idea that, even in our brokenness, we can find strength, purpose, and a path forward.

Through this book, I hope to honor my Tantra Master and rage out my energy into something constructive—a blessing for others who seek to navigate their own complexities. Together, we can cultivate a deeper understanding of our sexuality, embrace our authenticity, and foster connections that are rooted in respect and love. Let us embark on this journey together, reclaiming our energy and creating spaces where we can be better men—for ourselves and with our partner(s).

SPIRITUAL AND SEX JOURNEY

Much of the discussion in this section, and my personal belief, comes from Kemet teachings when discussing the tree of life. Here is where part of the Book's title was created with Ba (sex).

For those who have yet to read Metu Neter or any history of the African Tree of Life, Kamitian traditions understand the sphere of being all the way down to the sphere of living. Perched at the top of the tree in Spheres 1 through 3 is God, also known as BA. This sphere is represented by extraordinary beings such as Jesus, Buddha, and others who have dedicated their lives and significant time to the higher, who can speak with the higher, who can see the higher, and so much more. As stated in Metu Neter, consciousness on this level enables the person to realize that the self is one and the same as that which dwells in all things, as well as one with God. While most people in society will not be able to achieve this level, it is something to strive for. In order to get there, however, we need to raise the consciousness of those from the lower level of the tree, which is Sahu, to Ab.

Metu Neter urges us to reach for Ab, consisting of spheres 4 through 6 and which has familiar names such as Heru or Horus and Maat. This is an achievable level for society's consciousness, up from Sahu. Here, the conscious will not only remember and correspond to a celestial government but also perceive abstract principles underlying and uniting things and events in the world. My tribe has lifted many men to this level, and in an effort to maintain that code, I work to both keep myself at this level as well as lift others to it. This was and will continue to be my promise made in oath.

Sahu is the physical level at which we're born. Metu Neter states, " When our consciousness is focused in the Sahu part of the spirit, our mental perception is limited to the external side of things. We are able to recognize concrete specifics but not the abstract principles. Fully evolved people understand there is no such thing as "a medicine" or "a poison." All substances can be used medicinally or toxically according to their dosage. There is a level where some substance will poison and heal."

This was a simple example of the duality with which the Sahu-level consciousness can and will struggle. I feel spaces for men need to be created outside of this book, enabling us to discuss topics we may have missed or simply need a higher-level conversation to engage with at a higher level of consciousness. Before we can reach Ab from Sahu, we must start with the journey of understanding our true selves. That journey is best described in a book by Dr. Richard King.

Please enjoy the ideas in this book, but more importantly, put them into action in your life. Stay connected and access exclusive resources, along with a custom soundtrack designed to complement the book's sensual mood, by visiting www.backtothebasex.com.

CHAPTER 1
A MESSAGE TO BLACK MEN

MESSAGE FROM THE DOC...

I n the book Ancient Origin of African Biological Psychiatry, Dr. Richard King reports, "Black Dot is an ancient symbol for blackness, it is the black seed of all humanity, archetypes of humanity, the hidden doorway to the collective unconsciousness-darkness, the shadow, primeval ocean, chaos, the womb, doorway of life." Dr. King goes on to mention the history of a scientific investigation spanning over 300 thousand years and conducted by scientists who were Black in consciousness. They discovered and uncovered the fundamental nature of the hidden door to their souls and spirits—a doorway to advanced laws and rhythms within the black seed, feeding every dimension in space and time. He continues, "the black dot was found to be the hidden doorway to universal knowledge of the past, present, and future." Thus, Black people have started to awaken from their mental slavery by realizing and studying the histories of their origins dating back to their ancestors. King purports that today's reborn Black people, as mental masters, can focus the mind by embracing their historical blackness, developing a deep knowledge of their ancestry, and becoming affluent in the translation of ancient images that appear around the world, even in dreams, visions, and things that seem hard to imagine. This energy will serve as a motivator for becoming your "true self" and no longer denying the gifts with which you were born.

MESSAGE TO BLACK MEN

I'd be remiss if I didn't speak to the people who look like me, sound like me, grew up with me, and share goals of succeeding beyond our wildest imaginations. Even those who failed. I think about the people who played a vital role in my existence, helped shape my attitude, and challenged me throughout life. The very people I challenged, loved, and understood were in spaces that needed healing, but they weren't quite ready to take that journey.

I smile at the thought of the ones I know personally who are thriving in their life journeys. I smile at the ones who taught me about my wrongs—how I needed to not wrong another man for his mistakes but participate in his learning process to be better. I see the parallels that exist within us all and the challenges that divide us within the same breath. These are the factions that cause a leakage of energy. Division and groupthink are spaces that cause us to operate with little to no energy. I pray we can honor our ancestors together and build a strong bond, so we may thrive in our true selves and enjoy this lifetime before we travel to the next. I love and appreciate you from the deepest parts of my heart and soul, and I hope you find your true self.

However, I must challenge you during this journey. I challenge you to stop blaming external factors, much like I did in the past when it came to failures in my career, in relationships, with money, and within my own tribe. A key focus in order for you to rise above all the issues that have burdened you is to understand that issues with outside sources start within you. The very thing you blame or wish to improve is nothing more than another iteration of your internal space screaming to get out so it can be nurtured and validated.

At this moment, I hope you can stop the leakage of energy and begin your healing journey with self-talk, paying close attention to the quality of conversation you begin having with yourself. Is there self-doubt? Are there ands or buts? Is there a significant amount of shoulds within this conversation? If so, it's time to start patching up your leaking energy, strengthening your ability to use your life force for transmutation. We'll get to that later.

BEYOND THE SCRIPTS

Ronald L. Jackson II, the author of Scripting the Black Masculine Body, defined Black masculine scripts, deconstructed them, and then listed them in six parts: (1) exotic and strange, (2) violent, (3) incompetent and uneducated, (4) sexual, (5) exploitable, and (6) innately incapacitated. I like to learn through stories, so I'm going to share a true story of a Black man doing his best to live beyond the scripts, as we all do at some point in time. Below is the short story of Marcus, a Black man doing his best to live a good life despite seemingly having to navigate scripts in an effort to find himself. His personal concern is that the gazes of others might shape him into the man they want him to be instead of allowing him to live beyond the scripts, tapping into his true self and living a life defined by his own terms. Even when he is doing well, these spaces still challenge and shrink in certain areas of life.

MARCUS' STORY

In the bustling heart of Chicago, Marcus navigated life with a quiet strength, always aware of the narratives that threatened to define him. Each day was a new challenge, but Marcus faced them head-on, determined to craft his own story.

From a young age, Marcus felt the weight of being perceived as exotic. People often commented on his deep, rich skin as though it were an artifact to be admired from afar. The whispers and lingering gazes felt like chains. Yet, Marcus embraced his heritage and immersed himself in the history of jazz, the soulful melodies echoing the resilience of his ancestors. Cultural festivals became his stage, where he shared his story and learned from others, transforming strangeness into a tapestry of shared human experience.

The world seemed to expect anger from him, a stereotype Marcus resisted with every fiber of his being. At the gym, he sparred not with rage but with discipline, honing his body and mind. He joined a community mentorship program, channeling his energy into uplifting young men who, like him, sought a path away from the shadows of violence. Organizing workshops on conflict resolution, he taught the youth the power of words over fists. His calm demeanor and patience became a beacon of hope, gradually shifting perceptions in the neighborhood.

Academia was Marcus' sanctuary, a place where he shattered stereotypes through sheer determination. Despite assumptions about his intellect, he excelled in engineering, proving time and again that intelligence knows no color. Long nights in the library became routine, his mind a sponge for knowledge. His passion led him to a prominent tech firm where his innovations spoke louder than any prejudice. Determined to pave the way for others, Marcus initiated a scholarship fund for young Black students, ensuring they had access to the education and opportunities he had fought so hard to attain.

The hypersexualization of his identity was a burden Marcus carried silently. He valued deep connections and sought love that transcended physical attraction. In Maya, he found a partner who saw beyond these scripts, cherishing his kindness and intellect. Together, they built a relationship rooted in respect and understanding, sharing dreams and fears. Volunteering together, they taught workshops on healthy relationships and self-worth, striving to dismantle harmful stereotypes for future generations.

In the workplace, Marcus often felt the pressure of being seen as a tool rather than a teammate. Determined to change this, he advocated for fair treatment and equal opportunities, leading initiatives that highlighted the talents of underrepresented voices. Collaborating with colleagues, he helped create mentorship programs, fostering an environment of growth and support. Marcus' leadership was transformative, gradually shifting the company's culture to one of inclusivity and respect.

There were moments when societal narratives sought to diminish him —to suggest he was less capable simply because of who he was. However, Marcus knew his worth. He pushed through barriers not just for himself but for those who came after him. Emerging as a mentor and leader, he inspired others to defy the scripts that sought to confine them. Speaking at conferences and schools, he shared his journey and encouraged others to write their own narratives.

Every day, Marcus lived with intention, crafting a narrative of his own making. He was more than the scripts imposed upon him; he was a testament to resilience, a beacon of hope for all who dared to dream beyond the stories written for them. Marcus' life was an example of triumph over adversity and a reminder that the essence of a person cannot be captured by stereotypes. Instead, that essence is defined by courage, love, and the unyielding pursuit of a better future.

BLACK MAN STIGMAS

The belief that Black men are failures in bed—or contemptible in some ways related to sex and sexuality—would be reinforced in the minds of some of these men by a societal stigma that suggests such characteristics are peculiar to them. An individual once mentioned that the biggest issues Black men concurrently face from every community they identify with are those of racism and homophobia. Rejection, racism, internalized racism, historical and ongoing discrimination, anxiety, and judgment play a huge part in Black men's stigmas. Underlying biases about Black men often play out when they seek medical services, and this is only heightened when sexual activity is included in the equation. People tend to pick up sexual shame from the world around them, starting with the messages they receive as children from parents, churches, communities, and culture. Interestingly, most of these messages may not even be overt or direct. The majority of Black men have internalized shame about sex and their sexuality as a result of growing up in a culture that views our bodies, sex, and our sex parts as bad.

One thing that has made sexual shame so insidious is that people are unaware of their shame. The failure to identify and see it has made many people shy away from the topic. As a matter of fact, conversations regarding sexual shame are easily brushed under the rug, and as a result, a lot of people are unaware of how easy it is to obstruct their confidence and intimacy, let alone establish healthy relationships with self-pleasure, sex, and partners. That is the major reason we must first identify common thoughts, behavioral patterns, and feelings associated with sexual shame so we might tackle it effectively.

SEXUAL SHAME

Sexual shame springs up from negative evaluations of one's sexual identity, thoughts, behaviors, feelings, or attraction. Usually, sexual shame is associated with one's past sexual behaviors and experiences, and it often covers a wide range of topics including sex and sexuality, sexual desires, and intense personal elements of sexual identity that cannot be changed, such as gender and attraction. It has been established across a breadth of literature that there exists a need to understand what sexual shame entails as a whole.

FACTORS THAT INFLUENCE SEXUAL SHAME IN BLACK MEN

Religious Messages

Research has shown that religious or theologically conservative people feel profound guilt from violating moral expectations and codes after viewing pornography or engaging in non-martial lust and masturbation. There's a kind of limitation set by religious ideologies that emphasizes how sexual acts should take place within the institution of marriage, and this prevents individuals from exploring sexual identities, engaging in sexual behaviors, or making moves to understand the concept of contraception, safer sex, and abortion practices. The wide difference between internalized religious representation and one's own experiences of sexual desire may contribute to feelings of shame, guilt, and internalized conflict.

Indeed, Black men from conservative religious backgrounds seem to be at higher risk for experiencing sexual shame and relational distress as compared to their non-religious counterparts. Religious and cultural messages pertaining to sex and sexuality may carry undertones that convey gender-based assumptions and moral judgments that counter sex-positive approaches. These religious-based messages about sex and sexuality may additionally lead to feelings of sexual shame, as evidenced by the fact that the majority of sacred texts promote abstinence, position sex as dirty and dangerous, contain oppressive gender stereotypes, perpetuate rape myths, and avoid directly addressing issues related to sexual health and intimacy. Rigid teachings about sexual identity also permeate religious messages across various faiths. Strict adherence to heterosexual identities and monogamous partnerships exist in Muslim law and are notoriously grounded in the Bible Clobber passages, while traditionally marginalizing scriptures used out of context to condemn same-sex activity may create additional disparaging messages that promote the presence of sexual shame. Christian dogma conceptualizes same-sex behavior as diseased, perverse, sinful, and inferior. Consequently, lesbian, gay, bisexual, transgender, and queer (LGBTQ) individuals may experience internal and external conflict as they negotiate disparate religious and sexual identities.

These challenges may be especially marked for religious LGBTQ people of color, particularly those who reside along the Bible Belt in the United States, a geographical region associated with religion encompassing northern Texas to western North Carolina and stretching from Mississippi to Kentucky (Brunn, Webster, & Archer, 2011). Existing research has identified feelings of shame, guilt, inadequacy, trauma, and suicidality in LGBTQ persons who lack affirming religious messages (Hattie & Beagan, 2013; Sherry, Adelman, Whilde, & Quick, 2010). LGBTQ individuals may also experience rejection from their religious communities and family members (Barrow & Kuvalanka, 2011; Dahl & Galliher, 2012; Hattie & Beagan, 2013), which increases their likelihood of developing mental health symptoms and becoming homeless.

7

. . .

Social Messages

From an early age, children begin receiving messages about reproduction, their bodies, and sexual health. These internalized messages about sex, sexuality, and bodies may influence the development of sexual shame. Early messages girls receive about sexual health and reproduction have lasting impressions on their identity development, conceptualization of sexual activity, and relationships with their bodies across the lifespan. In addition, children who are punished or ridiculed for engaging in sexually curious behaviors often experience feelings of guilt and shame. The taboo nature of topics related to sex and sexuality often perpetuates the internalization of sexual shame. As a result, girls and women who have internalized the prohibited nature of sexual topics may be more likely to keep the details of sexual abuse hidden, which only serves to maintain and perpetuate feelings of sexual shame. Indeed, early messages from families of origin may lead to the stifling of natural sexual expression, exploration, and curiosity, resulting in ongoing experiences of sexual shame.

At the other end of the spectrum, boys and men are subjected to societal messages that communicate conflicting notions about the nature of sex, intimacy, and sexual expression. For example, boys and men exposed to societal messages that center on cis-heteronormativity may endorse attitudes that value sexual performance and aggression rather than vulnerability, communicating feelings, or enhancing intimacy. Boys and men may additionally become subjected to shaming messages when they are viewed by others as embodying traits perceived as feminine, such as expressing emotions, endorsing fairness and equity, and engaging in help-seeking behaviors. Following experiences of male sexual victimization, the endorsement of heteronormative scripts and toxic cultural messages about masculinity may perpetuate the presence of sexual shame in boys and men.

The experiences of sexual shame in men appear to be distinct from those of most women and may include specific aspects related to sexual inexperience distress, masturbation/pornography remorse, libido disdain, body dissatisfaction, dystonic sexual actualization, and sexual performance insecurity.

Counselors are therefore encouraged to adhere to a feminist, strength-based, and sex-affirming counseling approach that enables boys and men with sexual shame to reframe harmful patriarchal narratives surrounding masculinity. Technology has ushered in a new wave of sexual social messaging and provides novel opportunities for facilitating sexual health education. Increasing numbers of children, teens, and adults are looking to the Internet and social media as an informal source of sexuality education.

Several websites, mobile applications, and forms of game-based learning have emerged to improve the sexual health education of adolescents, which may help to address essential knowledge gaps young people may experience in the absence of formal, comprehensive sex education. For example, the gamification of sexual health education may be more motivating for adolescents compared to traditional teaching methods, and it can promote safer sexual behaviors through storytelling, roleplaying, and avatars. However, while there are benefits associated with the increased accessibility of sexuality-related information online, there are also increased opportunities for the spread of sexual misinformation. Individuals who access sexually explicit online content may be exposed to unrealistic and potentially harmful portrayals of sex, gender roles, objectification, sexual communication, and consent that may be internalized and contribute toward the development of sexual shame. While pornography and erotica may be useful tools in achieving sexual satisfaction and exploring erotic desire, there is a clear need for increased pornography literacy among viewers in light of growing evidence that the messages inherent in mainstream pornography can shape viewers' attitudes and expectations about sex, intimacy, and relationships in problematic ways. Porn literacy can be cultivated through curriculum and sex-positive conversations that empower viewers to interpret sexually explicit media while learning to identify and challenge their pre-existing notions, beliefs, and values about sex, bodies, and intimacy.

SOME OF THE SEXUAL SHAME BLACK MEN FACE

Black men face sexual shame in several forms, and we will be discussing some of them below.

Insecurity With the Self

Megwyn White, a sexologist, licensed sex coach, and director of education at sexual-wellness brand Satisfier mentioned that sexual shame often manifests as a disconnection from the self. She added that a major characteristic of sexual shame is a break in the natural flow of personal expression and experience of the body. Usually, Black men who are not comfortable with the appearance of their genitals are likely to experience a flood of intense self-judgment after sex or self-consciousness and body insecurity during sex. Some of these concerns include:

- Fear that you won't perform well in bed or satisfy your partner(s) sexually
- Poor body image, including concern over your weight
- Worry that your penis won't "measure up"
- Concern about ejaculating too early or taking too long to reach orgasm
- Anxiety about not being able to have an orgasm or enjoy the sexual experience

A Certain Physical Stature or Diminished Voice

Sexual shame can also present itself in how we carry ourselves. For instance, you may frequently cross your legs or arms, slouch, hunch your shoulders, or struggle to make or hold eye contact with your partner(s). White mentioned that there is a general inhibition to make sounds during sexual exploration, and as such, it will likely affect the voice. White added that the moment you feel uncomfortable expressing desires and needs during a sexual act, that can be categorized as shame too.

Sexual Dysfunction and Dissatisfaction

Sexual dysfunction and dissatisfaction in men often stem from barriers that disrupt the natural flow of sexual energy and arousal. When feelings of shame creep in, they can create a tangled web that obstructs desire, excitement, and the ability to achieve orgasm. It's important to recognize that a lack of arousal does not necessarily indicate shame; rather, it may result from a complex interplay of various factors affecting sexual response.

Additionally, shame can hinder open communication between partners, leading to misunderstandings that diminish sexual pleasure. When partners struggle to express their needs and desires, their intimacy may suffer, further complicating their sexual experiences. Addressing these emotional barriers and fostering honest dialogue can be crucial steps toward enhancing both satisfaction and overall sexual well-being.

THE BENEFITS OF OVERCOMING SEXUAL SHAME—AND HOW TO DO IT

Confronting and releasing sexual shame opens the door to a more fulfilling sexual experience, starting with the simple joy of pleasure. When individuals address their feelings of shame, they often find that their sexual responses improve, allowing them to move beyond dysfunction and experience heightened arousal and orgasm that may have been previously inhibited. This transformation not only enhances personal satisfaction but also enriches intimate connections with partners.

Identifying the root causes of sexual shame is a crucial first step in this journey. By recognizing specific activating events that trigger feelings of shame, individuals can create boundaries that protect their emotional well-being. This involves developing a plan to manage oneself, which can significantly reduce the leakage of sexual energy. Establishing a safe space for exploration and understanding allows for the healthy expression of desires and feelings, fostering an environment where pleasure can thrive.

Once boundaries are set and the problem is identified, the focus can shift toward using this vital sexual energy for personal healing and growth. Transmuting sexual energy into a healing component of self can lead to greater self-awareness and empowerment. This process not only boosts sexual confidence but also contributes to overall mental and emotional well-being.

The benefits of overcoming sexual shame are numerous. Individuals may experience increased intimacy with partners, enhanced sexual satisfaction, improved communication about desires, and a stronger sense of self-acceptance. Ultimately, addressing and releasing sexual shame paves the way for a more authentic and pleasurable sexual experience, fostering deeper connections and a healthier relationship with one's sexuality.

Overcoming sexual shame can lead to a wealth of benefits that positively impact various aspects of life. By confronting these feelings, individuals can reclaim their sexual identity and enhance their overall quality of life.

1. **Increased Sexual Satisfaction:** One of the most immediate benefits of overcoming sexual shame is heightened sexual satisfaction. When individuals shed feelings of shame, they often find it easier to engage in intimate experiences without fear or anxiety. This newfound freedom allows for greater exploration of desires and preferences, leading to more fulfilling sexual encounters.

2. **Improved Intimacy and Connection:** Releasing sexual shame fosters deeper emotional intimacy with partners. Open communication about desires, boundaries, and vulnerabilities becomes possible when shame is no longer a barrier. This can lead to stronger relationships, as partners feel more connected and understood, creating a safe space for both emotional and physical intimacy.

3. **Enhanced Self-Acceptance and Confidence:** Confronting sexual shame is closely tied to personal growth and self-acceptance. As individuals work through their feelings, they

often gain a better understanding of their own sexuality, leading to increased confidence. This self-assurance extends beyond the bedroom, positively affecting various areas of life, including personal relationships and professional interactions.

4. **Healthier Communication:** Overcoming sexual shame encourages healthier communication about sex and intimacy. Partners can discuss their needs, boundaries, and preferences openly, reducing misunderstandings and enhancing mutual satisfaction. This transparency fosters a culture of respect and support within relationships, allowing both partners to feel valued and heard.

5. **Greater Emotional Resilience:** Addressing sexual shame can also contribute to improved emotional resilience. As individuals learn to navigate and manage their feelings, they develop coping strategies that can be applied to other areas of life. This enhanced resilience helps individuals face challenges more effectively, leading to overall improved mental health.

6. **Liberation from Societal Norms:** Overcoming sexual shame allows individuals to break free from societal expectations and norms that dictate what is considered "appropriate" sexuality. This liberation encourages people to explore their unique desires without judgment, fostering a more authentic expression of self.

7. **Empowerment and Personal Growth:** Finally, the process of overcoming sexual shame can be a powerful catalyst for personal growth. Individuals may find themselves more open to self-exploration, leading to a deeper understanding of their values, desires, and boundaries. This empowerment can extend to other areas of life, inspiring individuals to pursue their passions and interests with renewed vigor.

Ultimately, overcoming sexual shame can lead to increased sexual satisfaction, improved intimacy, enhanced self-acceptance, healthier communication, greater emotional resilience, liberation from societal norms, and a profound sense of empowerment. By addressing these feelings, individuals can embrace their sexuality fully and enjoy richer, more fulfilling lives.

WAYS TO OVERCOME ISSUES THAT ARE SEXUALLY RELATED

Social expectations around sexual behavior can lead to sexual guilt and shame, regardless of gender or identity. However, this is something you can absolutely overcome. First, as a Black man, you need to know that irrespective of whether the stigma surrounding your sex or sexuality is true or false, it is not your fault. Simply having an awareness of your sex, your sexuality, and how it affects you can help you take reasonable steps toward countering any form of shame. Helpful tips are included below.

Practice Mindfully Accepting Sexual Thoughts

When you become more mindful and comfortable about your sexual thoughts, you become increasingly aware of and learn to accept them without judgment or guilt. In other words, you could actually think about smooching a big, well-rounded boob, sucking on it for minutes, and having the feeling of it placed on your head. You only need to remind yourself that your thoughts are normal and let them pass without criticizing yourself. You might even proceed to follow your thoughts with curiosity and explore what they suggest—an ecstatic and euphoric experience you'd like to have.

Read Up On Sex Positivity

Being positive about sex can help you counter sexual-related issues you may happen upon. Becoming more comfortable with the idea of sex as a healthy activity will help you walk through shame. You could begin by reading books or essays about sexual expression as a means of exploring sex positivity. You could also explore a series of pornographic content including independent or ethical porn, or you could familiarize yourself with sexual expression in films, art, and books. If you prefer toned-down scenes to erotica, you can find books and movies for your use, too.

Get Comfortable With Your Body

When you are ashamed of your sex and sexuality, it can affect how you feel about your body. You might tend to hide or desexualize your body rather than love and accept your physical self.

To increase your comfort with your own body, you might try:

- sleeping naked,
- listing five things you like about your body, and
- looking at yourself in the mirror naked.

Talk to Your Partner(s)

Opening the door to conversation with an understanding partner could work a lot of magic in terms of helping you feel more comfortable voicing your desires. You could start by saying something like, "I've never felt comfortable talking about or acknowledging what I like in bed. I want to improve, but it will take time." Again, mindfulness plays a cogent role during sex; it helps you recognize when you enjoy something and shields you against unwanted thoughts that could distract you. You can have a beautiful sexual experience this way.

Get Intimate in Other Ways

Learn how to be intimate without sexual intercourse. Give your partner(s) a sensual massage or take a warm bath together. Take turns pleasing each other with masturbation so you don't always have to feel pressured to perform sexually.

Exercise

Not only does working out make you feel better about your body, but it also improves your stamina in bed.

Talk to a Therapist

Make an appointment with a counselor or therapist who has experience treating sexual problems. Therapy can help you understand, reduce, or get rid of the issues that are causing you sexual performance anxiety. If you worry about premature ejaculation, for example, you can try some techniques that help you gain more control.

BREAKING THE CYCLE

Several factors or matters that have contributed to passing down misguided or harmful ideas about sexuality don't necessarily mean to cause harm most times. People simply share beliefs they've learned themselves. This can lead to different problems, especially when there is a repetition of this cycle. Hence, it is good to address this issue of shame pertaining to sex and sexuality in Black men.

You can also promote healthy ideas about sexuality by:

- teaching children what healthy romantic and sexual relationships look like,
- talking about sex honestly, in an age-appropriate way,
- exposing children to relationships between people of all genders and sexualities through real-life or media portrayals,
- providing affirming resources to LGBTQIA+ children, and
- teaching consent from an early age.

KEY TAKEAWAYS

For far too long, Black men have been shackled by oppressive stereotypes that seek to define their sexuality as aggressive, hedonistic, and animalistic. These damaging narratives, perpetuated by media and societal constructs, aim to strip away our humanity and reduce us to mere caricatures. It's time to challenge falsehoods and reclaim our identity with knowledge, pride, and pleasure.

We must examine the roots of stereotypes critically and ask ourselves this: Is it society or science that has shaped this distorted image of Black male sexuality? The truth is that these portrayals serve to confine us, limiting our potential and diminishing our diverse experiences. It's essential to dismantle these myths and embrace a narrative that honors our complexity and individuality.

Black men, like all individuals, deserve the freedom to define their identities beyond societal misconceptions. Embracing your sexuality should be an act of liberation, not one of shame or conformity to false narratives. To truly thrive, we must focus on holistic health—mental, physical, and emotional. Prioritize self-care and seek spaces where you can express your true self without judgment. Engage in open conversations about sexuality that celebrate diversity and individuality. By doing so, we reclaim our humanity and dismantle the myths that have long overshadowed our stories.

Remember, your worth is not determined by external perceptions but by your own understanding and acceptance of who you are. By embracing a healthy, authentic exploration of your sexuality, you pave the way for future generations to live free from the constraints of damaging stereotypes.

CHAPTER 2
SELF-CARE IS SEX-CARE

In modern manhood, where the daily grind often feels like a relentless treadmill of work, social expectations, and mind-numbing scrolling through social media, it's easy to overlook a crucial truth: Self-care is not just a luxury. Rather, it's essential for a fulfilling life—and a rewarding sex life. The pressures of living under a scarcity mindset, where we constantly feel there isn't enough time, energy, or resources, can be unhealthy and deter us from prioritizing self-care. This mindset often leads to stress and anxiety, which can negatively impact our relationships and personal well-being.

However, adopting an abundance mindset can transform this narrative, encouraging us to see opportunities where we once saw limitations. By embracing this perspective, we can cultivate a more balanced approach to life that allows for both personal growth and the enjoyment of healthy relationships. This balance is key to maintaining a vibrant and satisfying sexual connection with our partner(s).

Self-care is the secret sauce to not just surviving but thriving in every aspect, including the bedroom. It involves taking intentional steps to nurture your physical, emotional, and mental health. This might mean setting aside time for exercise, meditation, or simply enjoying a hobby. By focusing on self-care, you counteract the negative effects of a scarcity mindset, boost your sexual energy, and foster a deeper connection with your partner(s).

Investing in self-care also means recognizing the importance of rest and relaxation. In a world that often glorifies busyness, taking time to recharge can enhance your overall well-being, leading to improved mood and increased intimacy. By prioritizing self-care, you create a positive cycle that not only benefits you but also enriches your relationships.

So, grab your favorite beverage, kick back, and reflect on how integrating self-care into your daily routine can supercharge your well-being and your relationships. Embrace the abundance mindset and discover the profound impact it can have on your life, both inside and outside the bedroom.

UNDERSTANDING THE IMPORTANCE OF SELF-CARE IN MODERN LIFE

Let's face it: Modern life can sometimes feel like being trapped on a hamster wheel. You're running, running, running—yet you're not really going anywhere. To break free from this trance, here are five self-care practices that can enhance your health, deepen your connection with your partner(s), and rev up your sex drive:

1. **Regular Exercise**: No, we're not talking about grunting through some heavy lifting while desperately trying not to drop the weights on your toes. Find an activity you love, whether it's dancing like nobody's watching or trying out that martial arts class you've always been curious about. Exercise boosts your endorphins, which are basically nature's way of giving you a high-five. Plus, it helps with stamina, which is great for more than just running errands.
2. **Mindful Eating**: Put down that cold pizza from last week and start treating your body like the temple it is rather than a frat house. Nourish yourself with wholesome foods like avocados, dark chocolate, and oysters (yes, those aphrodisiac legends are based on some truth). Eating well fuels your energy levels and

keeps your libido from snoozing. Intention is the most important part here. Eating the right things and allowing said meal to follow its natural process uninterrupted is vital. Cut off the TV, engage with your partner(s), or have a great meal by yourself while letting the theatre of the mind take place for most of your meals. That's the best date—and a mindful one when you allow yourself to listen to your body and enjoy a hopefully healthy meal. Don't forget to add arugula and a good dose of spinach for nitric oxides in the body! Also, be sure to incorporate foods that burn fat alongside lowering your sugar intake. Fats and sugars not only have a dampening effect on the sexual response cycle but get harder to burn or manage as we age.

3. **Quality Sleep**: If you're like most men, you might think sleep is for the weak. Spoiler alert: It's not! Prioritizing quality sleep can improve your mood, cognitive function, and yes, even your libido. When you're well-rested, you're more likely to feel like a romantic hero instead of a grumpy troll. It's recommended to get 7 to 9 hours of sleep on average. This isn't realistic in a world of people working two to three jobs, so I recommend you stay above 5.5 hours of sleep a night to stave off any significant behavioral health issues, allowing the body to repair itself overnight. In addition, be sure to monitor erection quality in the morning. Morning wood is a sign of life and a natural response that lets you know your body is doing just fine. Quality sleep will help with that morning wood process, especially if you get restful sleep at night. Contact the nearest sleep clinic to assist with this process. For those gentlemen who have sleep apnea, the symptoms can be managed well with professional medical help.

4. **Mindfulness Practices**: Ever found yourself mindlessly scrolling through your phone while your partner is talking? (Yikes!) Mindfulness can help you connect more deeply with yourself and your loved ones. Spend a few moments each day practicing gratitude or meditation to reduce stress and enhance intimacy.

○ Belly Breathing: Rub your hands vigorously together, warming them—and hopefully with lotion on! Nobody wants ashy hands or cracked skin in this process. I recommend using coconut oil. Think about all the things that are troubling you, meaning all the issues that cause stress or rapid thoughts, and all the things you cannot seem to let go of. This is a time to either be free of thought or allow yourself to think freely through your troubles. Place one hand above your navel, typically in the area of the sacral chakra, with the other hand over your heart. Breathe in through your nose and fill your lungs. Visualize your energy rising up your spinal column as you inhale. Exhale while visualizing your energy going down the front half of your body, much like a beautiful waterfall. Rinse and repeat this simple breathing process with visualization.

○ Walk: Practice doing belly breathing and clear the mind. Now let's try taking a walk outside, shoes off. Walk heel to toe while engaging in your surroundings. If there's a tree, take time to notice it. Does it have a particular scent? Does it provide shade? How does it make you feel? If the environment is too noisy, this is the perfect opportunity to use the theatre of the mind with imagination and visualization. You can use headphones or no sound at all. Simply survey an area that brings peace and, with intention, focus on a particular object, enjoying the moment of it. Document your feelings, mood, and emotions afterward and over time to assess your sense of self.

5. **Social Interaction**: Make it a point to nurture your relationships not just with your partner(s) but with friends and family. Engaging in social activities can boost your mood and enrich your emotional life, directly impacting your sexual energy. Social interaction is important for quality of life; it's the motivation to increase quality relationships which boil down to two areas, namely love and connection. Have you noticed how your social interactions change based on your quality of love and connection with an individual or group of people?

Keeping this simple understanding in mind allows the individual to open up, engage with others, cultivate new experiences, and lean into gratitude.

THE CONNECTION BETWEEN SELF-CARE AND BREAKING THE TRANCE

We've all been there, caught in the whirlwind of work pressures, societal expectations, and the never-ending list of responsibilities that lead to poor health and lackluster intimacy. Self-care acts as a powerful antidote, helping you break free from the trance of daily distractions. It's like hitting the reset button on your life, allowing you to focus on what truly matters—like connecting with your partner(s) and unleashing your inner romantic.

SET THE STAGE FOR SEXUAL ENERGY WITH SELF-CARE

Now that we've set the groundwork, let's talk about how to specifically enhance your sexual energy through self-care.

Prioritizing Nutritious Eating Habits

What you put on your plate can significantly impact your performance in the bedroom. Here are three meals that will not only nourish your body but also tantalize your taste buds and boost your libido:

1. **Salmon with Quinoa and Asparagus**: Rich in omega-3 fatty acids, salmon boosts blood flow and supports heart health. Paired with quinoa (a protein powerhouse) and asparagus (loaded with vitamins), you've got a meal that's both delicious and energizing.
2. **Dark Chocolate-Covered Strawberries**: A classic for a reason! Dark chocolate is known to release endorphins, while strawberries are packed with vitamins that support sexual health. Plus, they make for a fun dessert to share with your partner(s)—talk about a sweet connection!
3. **Spicy Chickpea Bowl**: Chickpeas are a great source of protein and fiber, keeping you satisfied and energized. Toss them with

some spices, veggies, and a squeeze of lemon for an invigorating meal that's good for the body and the soul.

Embracing a self-care ritual is essential for personal well-being. These rituals allow you to reconnect with your inner self, promoting balance and harmony in your life. Practices like nostril breathing, qi-gong, meditation, and sun gazing can be transformative. They not only enhance your mental and emotional health but also improve your sexual vitality and presence, creating a more fulfilling intimate experience.

In our digitally dominated lives, taking the time for a digital detox is more important than ever. Unplugging from social media and digital spaces can greatly enhance your ability to be present with your partner(s). This presence is crucial for building intimacy and trust, leading to more satisfying relationships and, by extension, a more fulfilling sex life.

Creating a self-care plan that incorporates regular hygiene practices is vital for lasting change. Simple acts such as washing and grooming your beard, caring for your nails, hair, and skin, and scheduling regular medical check-ups play a significant role in maintaining health and trust in relationships. These practices not only contribute to a positive self-image but also demonstrate respect and consideration for your partner(s), enhancing both emotional and physical intimacy.

ENHANCING INTIMACY THROUGH DIGITAL DETOX AND HYGIENE

In our hyper-connected world, the constant barrage of notifications and information can be overwhelming. This digital noise often detracts from our ability to be fully present with those who matter most—typically our partner(s). Engaging in a regular social media detox can dramatically improve your relationships. By setting aside time each day to unplug, you allow yourself to focus on genuine, face-to-face interactions. This increased presence fosters deeper emotional connections, leading to more satisfying and meaningful intimate experiences.

DIGITAL DETOX FOR BETTER INTIMACY

1. **Set Boundaries**: Designate specific times of day to be free from digital devices. Use this time to engage in activities with your partner(s), such as cooking together or taking a walk.
2. **Create Tech-Free Zone**s: Establish areas in your home, like the bedroom or dining room, where devices are not allowed. This encourages communication and connection without distractions.
3. **Mindful Consumption**: Be selective about your digital content. Follow profiles that inspire and uplift, and limit exposure to those that cause stress or anxiety.
4. **Weekly Disconnect**: Allocate one day a week to completely unplug. Use this time to explore new hobbies, meditate, or simply enjoy your partner's company without digital interference.

COMPREHENSIVE HYGIENE ROUTINE FOR MEN

Maintaining a clean and healthy body is crucial for preventing infections and ensuring a positive experience for both you and your partner(s). Here's a detailed hygiene plan:

1. **Daily Showering**:
   ○ Use a gentle, pH-balanced body wash to cleanse your skin.
   ○ Pay special attention to intimate areas, ensuring thorough cleaning and rinsing.
2. **Facial Hair Care**:
   ○ Wash your beard daily using a mild shampoo to remove food particles and bacteria.
   ○ Condition regularly to keep the hair soft and reduce irritation during close contact.
3. **Nail Hygiene**:
   ○ Trim your nails regularly to prevent the accumulation of dirt and bacteria. This is especially important when using hands for solo or partnered sex. Dirt under the nails can

impact micro tears in the skin or affect your partner's PH balance.

- Clean under the nails daily and consider regular manicures to maintain neatness and present yourself with an understanding of self-care, leading to opportunities to engage more.

4. **Oral Hygiene**:
   - Brush your teeth at least twice a day and floss to prevent gum disease and bad breath. Good oral hygiene is essential for maintaining heart health. Also, if there's any current infection in the mouth, you're putting your partner(s) at risk of being exposed to the infection when practicing oral sex.
   - Use mouthwash to further eliminate bacteria. Be sure to research the mouthwash you select and give yourself time to use it. Statistics show that certain mouthwash formulas can contribute to ED over time.

5. **Skin Care**:
   - Moisturize daily to maintain healthy skin and prevent dryness, penis included! Hydrate your warrior. I again recommend coconut oil, as it's a substance with health benefits for the skin and which works well with your partner's yoni in most cases. Hopefully, she's not allergic, but if so, then disregard that comment.
   - Exfoliate weekly to remove dead skin cells and promote smooth skin.

6. **Regular Medical Check-Ups**:
   - Schedule annual check-ups to monitor overall health.
   - Stay informed about vaccinations and preventive screenings.

By incorporating these digital detox strategies and hygiene practices, you create an environment conducive to deeper intimacy and trust. Not only does this enhance your relationship, but it also demonstrates respect and care for both your own well-being and that of your partner(s).

KEY TAKEAWAYS

Here are some key takeaways from the passage:

1. Self-Care as Essential: Self-care isn't a luxury; it's vital for a fulfilling life and a healthy sex life. Prioritizing self-care can enhance overall well-being and intimacy.
2. Exercise: Regular physical activity boosts endorphins, enhancing mood and stamina. Choose activities you enjoy to make exercise a sustainable habit.
3. Mindful Eating: Nourish your body with healthy foods to maintain energy and libido. Be intentional with meals, focusing on wholesome, nutrient-rich options.
4. Quality Sleep: Sufficient restful sleep improves mood, cognitive function, and libido. Aim for 7 to 9 hours, but ensure at least 5.5 hours to maintain health.
5. Mindfulness Practices: Engage in mindfulness to reduce stress and improve connection with yourself and others. Techniques like belly breathing and mindful walking can enhance awareness and presence.
6. Social Interaction: Cultivate relationships with friends, family, and partner(s) to boost your mood and emotional well-being, which positively impacts sexual energy.
7. Importance of Self-Care and Hygiene:
   - Regular hygiene practices, including beard grooming, nail care, and skin care, are essential for health and relationship trust.
   - These practices enhance self-image and demonstrate respect for your partner(s), boosting intimacy.
8. Digital Detox for Enhanced Relationships:
   - Reducing digital distractions improves presence and fosters deeper emotional connections.
   - Strategies include setting device-free times, creating tech-free zones, and mindful content consumption.
9. Comprehensive Men's Hygiene Routine:

- ◦ Daily showering and facial hair care prevent infections and maintain cleanliness.
- ◦ Nail and oral hygiene are crucial for preventing bacteria spread and maintaining health.
- ◦ Regular moisturizing and exfoliating promote healthy skin, while medical check-ups ensure overall well-being.

10. Building Deeper Intimacy:
- ◦ A digital detox and a robust hygiene routine create an environment of trust and care.
- ◦ These practices show respect for oneself and one's partner(s), enhancing both physical and emotional intimacy.

CHAPTER 3
CAN EMOTIONAL IQ AND INTIMACY IMPROVE MY PERFORMANCE?

Have you ever experienced the profound depths of love? Or, to frame it differently, have you ever shared an intimate bond with someone, fostering a deep emotional attachment? If your answer is no, there's no cause for concern. Simply roll with me on this sexploration; how you engaged with yourself and others in your old experiences will help you create new, beautiful ones. Conversely, if you have experienced such connections, reflect on how those moments made you feel. You likely found yourself yearning for frequent communication and closeness, desiring to spend quality time together and engage in physical intimacy. This dynamic exemplifies the intersection of intimacy and emotional intelligence (EI), both of which significantly contribute to enhancing your performance in the bedroom. Regrettably, many individuals conflate EI with merely possessing feelings for another person. To elucidate this concept, I will define EI and examine its role in enriching intimate relationships, beginning with five essential components: self-awareness, emotional regulation, motivation, empathy (romantic, cognitive, and affective), and social skills. With these five levels, you will have a deeper insight into how you manage yourself and function daily. A few times each week, evaluate yourself in the here and now with these five steps. Work yourself up to assessing yourself daily and plot your findings in a journal. Notice how you've changed or stayed the same over the course of a month. Take particular notice as to how you engage in self-care or the lack thereof. Notice how you engage in the experience of enjoying others around you as well as the desire to make love or have sex. What did you notice about yourself?

SELF-AWARENESS

Self-awareness is the ability to recognize and understand your own emotions, thoughts, and values. In the context of love and intimacy, being self-aware helps individuals understand their desires, fears, and boundaries. This awareness allows for more honest communication with your partner(s), leading to deeper connections and a more fulfilling sexual experience. When you know what you want and need, you can articulate it to your partner(s), enhancing mutual satisfaction.

Assess self-awareness with five steps using self-talk. The five areas are: physical, emotional, sexual, intimate, and spiritual. Engage in the five areas using the "I feel" statements. This allows you to practice bringing your consciousness from your mind and into your body. Assess how you feel in these areas in the here and now.

EMOTIONAL REGULATION

Emotional regulation involves managing your emotions in a healthy way. This is crucial in intimate relationships where feelings can run high. By regulating your emotions, you can maintain composure during conflicts, communicate effectively, and avoid destructive behaviors. This stability fosters a safe environment for intimacy in which partners feel comfortable expressing themselves and exploring their desires without fear of judgment or reactivity. Consider using an anger log to assess your triggers, thoughts, body signals, actions, and outcomes. Picture yourself in the past, present, and future while creating new and healthy outcomes in all of those experiences.

Techniques for Emotional Regulation:

- **Mindful Breathing**: Harness the power of the breath as an anchor for presence and calm. By directing attention to the rhythmic flow of inhalation and exhalation, we create space between stimulus and response, allowing emotions to arise and pass without becoming entangled in their grip.
- **Grounding Practices**: Connect with the present moment through grounding techniques such as mindful walking, body scanning, or sensory awareness. By anchoring ourselves in the here and now, we cultivate stability and resilience in the face of emotional turbulence.
- **Emotional Expression**: Find healthy outlets for emotional expression, whether through journaling, art, movement, or conversation. By giving voice to our feelings in constructive ways, we release pent-up energy and gain clarity and perspective on our emotional landscape.
- **Cognitive Reframing**: Challenge unhelpful thought patterns and cognitive distortions that fuel emotional distress. By reframing negative beliefs and shifting perspectives, we empower ourselves to reinterpret situations in a more balanced and adaptive light.
- **Self-Compassion Practices**: Cultivate a compassionate attitude toward ourselves in moments of emotional struggle. By offering kindness, understanding, and acceptance to our own inner experiences, we soothe the wounded parts of ourselves and foster resilience in the face of adversity.

MOTIVATION

Motivation refers to the drive to engage in healthy relationships rather than unhealthy ones. Individuals with high EI are generally more motivated to invest in their relationships, recognizing the benefits of love and intimacy. This motivation stems from a desire for personal growth and connection, which can lead to more passionate and fulfilling sexual experiences. In contrast, those lacking this motivation may find themselves embroiled in toxic relationships that can hinder intimacy and overall satisfaction.

EMPATHY (ROMANTIC, COGNITIVE, AND AFFECTIVE)

Empathy is the ability to understand and share the feelings of another. In romantic contexts, empathy can be categorized into three types:

- **Romantic Empathy**: Understanding your partner's emotional state and responding to it, fostering connection and intimacy.
- **Cognitive Empathy**: The ability to understand your partner's perspective and feelings, which is essential for effective communication and conflict resolution.
- **Affective Empathy**: Experiencing your partner's emotions as if they were your own, which deepens emotional bonds and enhances sexual experiences by creating a sense of unity and understanding.

SOCIAL SKILLS

Social skills encompass the abilities needed to interact effectively with others. In intimate relationships, strong social skills enable partners to communicate openly, resolve conflicts, and express affection. Good social skills also help in reading nonverbal cues, which is crucial during intimate moments. By fostering a positive and open atmosphere, partners can enhance their emotional connection, leading to more satisfying sexual experiences.

UNDERSTANDING EMOTIONAL INTELLIGENCE

One of my earliest lessons as a student of Master Yao, Founder of the Grand Trine Organization and my mentor, was recognizing the profound benefits and strengths derived from cultivating robust relationships with women. We explored the exquisite harmony inherent in the interplay between masculine and feminine energies, emphasizing the importance of fostering strong, healthy partnerships.

Significant portions of our discussions were dedicated to analyzing the activating events that lead to failed relationships, as well as the behaviors that give rise to unhealthy thoughts and emotions. Such detrimental mindsets often precipitate poor actions and decisions, resulting in a disbursement of sexual energy.

We further examined the detrimental effects of energy leakage, which diminishes one's vitality and hampers the ability to harness this potent force for healing and to positively influence both one's own life and that of others. Maintaining a high level of EI enables individuals to transmute and utilize this energy for their prosperity. When I refer to prosperity, I'm not referring to financial wealth; I'm discussing the reality of nurturing healthy and trusting relationships, achieving high performance at work, and caring for the physical, energetic, and spiritual aspects of oneself.

Unbeknownst to me at the time, Master Yao was not only a Tantra Master but also an unofficial yet highly trained behavioral specialist. In their 2004 study, Brackett, Mayer, and Warner examined EI and its relation to everyday behaviors, particularly concerning academic performance and five critical components: neuroticism, extroversion, openness to experience, agreeableness, and conscientiousness. Their findings indicated that women exhibited significantly higher EI compared to men. This disparity contributed to men experiencing a lower quality of life, resulting in poor decision-making, diminished work output, strained relationships, and overall subpar performance across the identified domains.

EI encompasses the capacity to understand, express, and regulate one's emotions. It extends beyond mere emotional expression to include the interpretation and response to others' emotions with empathy—romantically, affectively, and cognitively. EI equips individuals to discern when someone is unprepared to engage in conversation, play, or laughter. For instance, consider the discomfort of wanting solitude while someone enthusiastically describes a captivating party or the frustration of seeking rest while being urged to play soccer. EI enables one to perceive and respond appropriately to the emotions of others.

Many overlook the significance of EI, which contributes to the challenges encountered by otherwise intelligent individuals in corporate environments. While some individuals possess a natural inclination toward high EI, others acquire it through life experiences.

EI enhances one's ability to accurately perceive emotions, facilitating an understanding of non-verbal cues such as facial expressions and body language. It empowers individuals to utilize their emotions constructively. By accurately perceiving emotions, one can respond thoughtfully rather than impulsively. For instance, when faced with a partner's anger, EI allows for an interpretation of its underlying causes —it may stem from dissatisfaction with one's communication style or external stressors. EI encourages one to avoid assuming that the emotional turmoil is solely a reflection of oneself; it may indeed be related to the other person's experiences.

The ability to regulate one's emotions represents a vital component of EI. How one manages feelings of happiness, sadness, anger, or frustration speaks volumes about their level of EI.

Moreover, EI significantly enhances one's romantic and interpersonal relationships. It fosters the ability to pause and reflect before reacting. An emotionally intelligent person recognizes that emotions, while powerful, are transient. For instance, if a partner's actions provoke displeasure, EI enables one to express feelings without resorting to shouting or excessive displays of frustration. When anger arises, EI teaches individuals to refrain from projecting that anger onto others.

An emotionally intelligent individual can cultivate intimacy with their partner(s) by ensuring that their actions are guided not solely by emotion but by thoughtful consideration. EI facilitates calmness in moments of emotional upheaval, averting potential conflicts that could escalate into more serious issues within relationships.

Furthermore, EI fosters greater self-awareness. It not only enables an understanding of others' feelings but also deepens one's insight into one's own emotions. By identifying the factors contributing to one's emotional state, individuals can effectively address underlying issues. For example, if anger arises due to a partner's lack of attention, EI aids in recognizing that addressing the attention issue can dissolve the anger. This separation of the issue from the individual fosters intimacy, whereas drifting away from a partner in anger can severely impact the relationship and the intimacy it entails.

Additionally, EI cultivates empathy. It allows individuals to place themselves in another's position, feeling what they feel. Empathy informs one's reactions. For instance, if a partner declines a sexual advance, EI prompts the exploration of the reasons behind the rejection rather than jumping to unfounded conclusions. Perhaps the partner had a stressful day or experienced discomfort. By empathizing, one can approach the situation with understanding rather than resentment, ultimately strengthening intimacy.

HOW EMOTIONAL INTELLIGENCE AND INTIMACY ENHANCE YOUR SEX LIFE

For many men, when they feel that their sexual needs are not being met or that the spark in their sex life has dimmed, they often assume the solutions to their problems are purely physical. While physical intimacy is undoubtedly important, it is equally vital to recognize that a fulfilling sexual relationship also requires engagement of the mind and spirit. EI plays a crucial role in this dynamic, as it fosters deeper connections and enhances intimacy between partners.

THE ESSENCE OF EMOTIONAL INTELLIGENCE IN RELATIONSHIPS

EI includes the ability to recognize, understand, and manage one's own emotions while also being attuned to the emotions of others. For men, developing EI is a transformative journey that can lead to becoming what I term "sensual men." These men are not only aware of their own feelings but also possess the ability to empathize with their partner(s), creating a nurturing environment for intimacy to flourish.

BUILDING EMOTIONAL CONNECTIONS

At the foundation of any romantic relationship lies emotional attachment. Healthy love and connection serve as the anchor in these partnerships, fostering an environment in which partners feel secure and valued. Sensual men prioritize building this emotional connection, which can significantly enhance their sex lives. By engaging in open and honest communication, they create a space where partners can express their desires, fears, and needs without judgment.

UNDERSTANDING AND EMPATHY

EI allows sensual men to develop a deeper understanding of their partner's emotional states. This sensitivity enables them to respond appropriately to their partner's needs, both in and out of the bedroom. For instance, a sensual man can discern when his partner is feeling stressed or disconnected and can address those feelings with empathy and support. This attentiveness not only strengthens their emotional bond but also enhances their physical intimacy, as partners feel understood and cared for.

CREATING INTIMACY BEYOND THE PHYSICAL

Intimacy is a multifaceted experience that goes beyond physical touch. Sensual men understand that emotional intimacy is just as critical, if not more so, than physical intimacy in cultivating a satisfying sex life. They invest time in nurturing their relationship through shared experiences, active listening, and affectionate gestures. By creating a strong emotional foundation, they enable their partner(s) to feel safe and desired, leading to enhanced sexual chemistry.

THE IMPORTANCE OF VULNERABILITY

For many men, vulnerability can be daunting. However, sensual men recognize that being emotionally open is a strength rather than a weakness. By allowing themselves to be vulnerable, they invite their partner(s) to do the same, fostering a deeper level of trust and intimacy. This mutual vulnerability can lead to more passionate and fulfilling sexual experiences, as partners feel free to explore their desires without fear of judgment.

COMMITMENT TO GROWTH AND EFFORT

EI is not a static trait; it requires ongoing effort and commitment. Sensual men are dedicated to personal growth and improving their emotional awareness. They understand that maintaining a vibrant sex life requires continuous effort, both in terms of understanding themselves and being attuned to their partner's evolving needs. This commitment to growth helps sustain the passion and excitement in their relationships.

In summary, EI is a powerful tool that can help men become better lovers, transforming them into sensual men. By prioritizing emotional connections, understanding their partner(s), embracing vulnerability, and committing to growth, these men can enhance both their emotional and sexual intimacy. Ultimately, a fulfilling sex life is not solely about physical encounters but also the profound emotional bonds that enrich those experiences. By investing in EI, men can reignite the fire in their relationships and create a lasting, passionate connection with their partner(s).

HOW TO IMPROVE YOUR EMOTIONAL INTELLIGENCE

Now that we've acknowledged the undeniable importance of EI, you might be pondering the burning question: How do I actually improve my emotional IQ? Some folks seem to waltz through life with an innate grasp of emotions, while others are like confused puppies trying to navigate a maze of feelings. Fear not! Here are some tips to help you boost your EI, provided you're willing to put in the effort—because sadly, emotional growth doesn't come with a free trial.

Listen Up!

First things first: If you want to enhance your emotional skills, you need to do some serious listening. Understanding others' emotions starts with the fine art of eavesdropping—uh, I mean, listening. What if they're not saying anything, you ask? Well, communication isn't just about words; it's a rich tapestry woven with both verbal and non-verbal threads. Pay attention to body language and facial expressions, because they can tell you more than a thousand words, and sometimes they say even more than your in-laws at Thanksgiving. When you tune in to these cues, consider what might be stirring the emotional pot for them.

Put Yourself in Their Shoes (But Not Literally)

Listening is just the beginning. Next up is the grand sport of empathy. To truly understand someone, you must learn to walk a mile in their shoes—preferably without stepping on any toes. Empathy isn't a magical gift bestowed upon you at birth but a skill to be practiced. Imagine how you would feel or react if you were in their position. This practice will not only enhance your emotional intelligence but also improve your responses to life's many curveballs.

Reflect, Don't React!

Understanding emotions is one thing, but acting on them wisely is another. Take a moment to reflect on times when your emotions led the charge in your decision-making. Did you react like a deer caught in the headlights, or did you navigate the situation with grace? Also, consider how others' emotions might have influenced their reactions. A little self-reflection can go a long way in helping you respond rather than react, being like a Zen master instead of a headless chicken.

Questions Are Your Best Friends

To elevate your EI, become the curious cat of your social circle—minus the unfortunate nine lives. Ask questions! Whether it's about your own feelings or those of others, inquiry is key. Why are you feeling a certain way? What's behind someone else's quirky behavior? Sometimes, the answers lie in the most unexpected places. Remember, asking questions is not just a way to gather information; it's also a means to build connections and deepen understanding.

Let's wrap this up with a bow: EI is essential for fostering intimacy in your relationships, including that oh-so-important aspect of your love life. When you master the art of emotional understanding, you'll find yourself more adept at responding to both your own feelings and those of your partner(s). And when both of you are emotionally intelligent, navigating the ups and downs of intimacy becomes a whole lot easier —like finding the remote control in the couch cushions.

KEY TAKEAWAYS

- Intimacy and EI are key ingredients for a satisfying bedroom performance.
- EI helps you understand, express, and control your emotions— no more emotional rollercoasters!
- It enhances self-awareness, making you the insightful sage of your own life.
- It fosters intimacy with your partner(s), like a fine wine aging over time.
- It equips you to respond appropriately to your partner's emotions, ensuring smoother sailing through emotional storms.
- EI is not just a personal endeavor; it's a team sport!

CHAPTER 4
A NEW PERSPECTIVE ON LOVEMAKING

The world is a rich tapestry of individuals woven from various backgrounds, races, and socioeconomic factors that shape our experiences—in both life and intimacy. Our views on sex are as varied as the ingredients in my favorite Louisiana gumbo, where a robust roux enhances the flavor, symbolizing the diverse perspectives we hold about life itself. Each day, we navigate a maze of complex thoughts and decisions aimed at achieving a fulfilling life, especially in the nuanced realm of lovemaking.

One intriguing idea is the common perception that men are inherently simple creatures. At what point did we reduce men to a single scoop of vanilla ice cream—pleasant but lacking depth? The journey to manhood is anything but straightforward; it requires navigating a challenging course of growth just to reach the starting line of existence. Life is filled with complexities at every stage of this journey.

Having established that every individual embarks on a detailed and often challenging path to becoming their current selves, some with vibrant personalities and others less expressive, should we continue to oversimplify men? Or should we take on the more difficult yet rewarding challenge of understanding them on a deeper level? When our partners recognize the intricacies behind the exterior of masculinity, we can foster better understanding, connection, and ultimately, more fulfilling lovemaking.

However, let's not assign blame solely to women for any perceived lack of connection. The blame game is as futile as trying to catch smoke with your bare hands. The reality is that relationships resemble a complex dance—a tango where partners contribute to the rhythm, often without awareness. When misunderstandings occur, it's easy to fall into the trap of blaming one another, but that rarely leads to meaningful solutions.

Instead of casting blame, let's consider the factors that shape our perceptions of each other. Cultural narratives, societal expectations, and personal experiences significantly influence how we view our partner(s). If a woman perceives her male partner(s) as "simple," this may have arisen from past experiences, stereotypes reinforced by media, and societal portrayals of masculinity. While this doesn't justify the oversimplification, it does provide important context.

Men are often socialized to be stoic and less expressive, creating an illusion of simplicity. If we, as men, don't engage in open discussions about our feelings, desires, and complexities, how can we expect our partner(s) to see beyond the surface? The responsibility lies with us to create a safe space for dialogue, where emotions can flow freely and vulnerabilities can be shared without fear of judgment.

Moreover, understanding is a mutual endeavor. Just as we strive to comprehend the intricacies of womanhood and the factors influencing their perceptions, we must encourage our partners to explore the complexities of masculinity. This shared journey of discovery replaces blame with curiosity and allows empathy to flourish.

So rather than pointing fingers, let's extend our hands and create space for our partners. Let's invite them to join us in this exploration, peeling back the layers of our experiences and aspirations. After all, love and intimacy flourish through connection, understanding, and a willingness to embrace each other's complexities. When we approach our relationships with this mindset, we transform lovemaking from a mere act into a profound expression of our interconnected journeys.

MYTHS ABOUT A MAN'S SEX LIFE

Before we dive into the perspectives of men, I'd like to discuss the myths. It's how I process people and the social norms that guide us: by addressing myths and ruling them out. With that said, society is fond of generalizing the sex lives of men based on personal experiences, ideas, and beliefs, often leading to a cacophony of misconceptions that can distort our true selves. These perspectives frequently provide a skewed representation, painting men as either insatiable beasts or emotionally detached figures, neither of which encapsulates the multifaceted nature of masculinity. Furthermore, some men develop their own notions about their peers, influenced by whispers of triumphs and failures or the ever-present cloud of rumor. This creates a feedback loop where insecurity breeds judgment and judgment perpetuates misunderstanding.

Yet, amidst these societal narratives, several myths persist that hinder our progress toward a deeper understanding of ourselves and our partners. For instance, the idea that men are always ready for sex can lead to a dangerous oversimplification of male desire, ignoring the nuances of emotional connection and individual circumstances. Similarly, the belief that men should be dominant in the bedroom can stifle vulnerability, leaving many feeling pressured to conform to an unrealistic standard instead of embracing the beauty of mutual exploration.

These myths not only misrepresent the truth but also impede our journey toward more fulfilling love-making experiences. When men internalize these societal beliefs, it can create a barrier to authentic communication and emotional intimacy. Instead of viewing ourselves through the lens of these constructs, we should strive to dismantle them. By acknowledging the complexities of our desires and the importance of connection, we can embark on a more enriching love-making journey with our partners.

In doing so, we not only empower ourselves but also foster a healthier dialogue about masculinity and sexuality. Let's create a space where vulnerability is celebrated, where myths are debunked, and where men can feel liberated to explore their desires without the weight of societal expectations hanging over them.

PERSPECTIVE 1: MEN ALWAYS WANT SEX

Men always want sex? It's a notion as simplistic as thinking a Swiss Army Knife is just a fancy butter knife. Sure, many men do indeed have a hearty appetite for intimacy like a ravenous raccoon at a midnight buffet, but this single-minded portrayal overlooks the intricate design of male desire, anticipation, and life's many, many priorities.

Let's be honest: While some men might have a sex drive rivaling that of a hamster on a caffeine drip, for most, sexual desire is just one thread in the elaborate quilt of their existence. Picture, if you will, a man contemplating life's mysteries—the meaning of happiness, the intricacies of quantum physics, or why socks always disappear in the dryer. Amidst these profound thoughts, yes, a fleeting thought about sex may pop up, akin to a cat jumping onto a keyboard. Unexpected and a little chaotic, but certainly not the sole focus.

Men are not just walking hormones; they are multifaceted beings with aspirations that range from mastering the perfect pancake flip to understanding why their favorite sports team is perpetually underwhelming. So, while it's true that sexual desire forms part of their lives, let's not forget the existential crises, the quest for the ideal pizza topping, and the noble pursuit of finding the TV remote. In this grand theater of life, sex is just one act—albeit a particularly popular one—amidst a myriad of others, each vying for attention in the grand performance of manhood.

PERSPECTIVE 2: THE SEX IS BETTER WHEN THE MAN DELAYS HIS ORGASM FOR A LONGER TIME

Cultural Expectations: The notion that longer sexual encounters equate to better sex is deeply ingrained in cultural narratives. Many portrayals across media suggest that prolonged sessions are the gold standard for sexual satisfaction, often emphasizing endurance and stamina as markers of masculinity. This belief can lead to unrealistic expectations for both men and their partner(s).

Associations with Intimacy: There's a common belief that longer sex signifies deeper emotional connection and intimacy. The idea is that the time spent together during extended sessions fosters a stronger bond. While this can be true in some cases, it overlooks the fact that intimacy can be achieved in various forms and durations.

Diversity of Preferences: Just as individuals have different preferences for food or music, sexual preferences vary widely among men. Some may genuinely enjoy longer sessions, while others might find shorter encounters equally satisfying. The idea that all men prefer prolonged sexual experiences fails to account for this diversity.

Quality Over Quantity: The quality of the sexual experience often matters more than the duration. Factors such as emotional connection, mutual pleasure, and communication can significantly enhance the experience, regardless of how long it lasts. A passionate, brief encounter can foster intimacy just as effectively as a longer session.

Quickies: Short sessions can be incredibly rewarding and fulfilling. They offer spontaneity, excitement, and a break from routine, which can enhance desire and intimacy. Engaging in shorter encounters doesn't diminish the quality of the relationship. Rather, they can introduce variety and keep the sexual dynamic fresh.

Physical and Emotional Well-being: Sometimes, practical considerations—like time constraints or fatigue—make longer sessions impractical. Men, like anyone else, may have days when they prefer a quick pleasurable experience. This preference does not reflect laziness or lack of commitment; it simply acknowledges the realities of life.

Communication and Connection: Open communication between partners about desires and preferences is crucial. Understanding each other's needs can lead to more satisfying experiences, whether long or short. Discussing what feels good and what partners enjoy can enhance intimacy and pleasure.

Variety is Key: Embracing a range of sexual experiences—both long and short—can enrich a relationship. Variety can help partners explore different aspects of their sexuality, fostering a deeper understanding of each other's desires and preferences.

Redefining Success: Shifting the focus from duration to the overall experience can redefine what success in the bedroom looks like. Success can be measured by feelings of connection, satisfaction, and mutual enjoyment rather than simply the clock.

The belief that sex is inherently better when a man delays his orgasm for a longer time overlooks the complexities of human sexuality. Men, like everyone else, can enjoy a full spectrum of sexual experiences, from quick encounters to extended sessions. By recognizing that satisfaction comes in various forms and durations, we can foster a more open and inclusive understanding of intimacy. Ultimately, the goal should be mutual pleasure and connection, regardless of how long it lasts.

PERSPECTIVE 3: THE BIGGER THE PENIS, THE BETTER THE SEX

Ah, the age-old debate: Does size really matter? For many, the mere mention of penis size can evoke a symphony of chuckles, gasps, and the occasional tear. Men have faced ridicule from both women and fellow men—because apparently, the length of one's appendage is a topic of great philosophical importance. But let's not forget that satisfaction isn't solely determined by dimensions. In fact, partners can find pleasure in a spectrum of sizes, from the "Oh my, that's charming!" to the "Lights out, folks!" Variety is the spice of life—unless you're considered a size queen, in which case, hopefully you find your well-endowed man.

But is this obsession with size perhaps a distraction from deeper issues? Could it be that we're missing the vital ingredient of genuine connection in our relationships—or, when the mood strikes, in our consensual escapades outside of them? The root of this conundrum often lies in a lack of anatomical education, an absence of top-notch sex education programs, and the unfortunate propensity for partners to measure their pleasure against societal norms rather than their own unique experiences.

Interestingly, the average male member measures in at a modest 5 to 6 inches, which, as it turns out, is quite sufficient to reach that elusive G-spot. So, perhaps instead of fretting over measurements, we should focus on understanding our bodies, pleasure, desire, and the same of our partner(s). After all, as they say, when it comes to pleasure, it's not about the size of the ship but the motion of the ocean—and who wouldn't want to ride those waves?

PERSPECTIVE 4: MEN ALWAYS WANT TO BE IN CHARGE DURING SEX

While it might be a common trope that men always want to be in charge during sex, let's not paint with such a broad brush. Sex isn't a battlefield, after all—there's no need for a general to sound the charge! In reality, many men initiate intimacy, which can create the illusion that they're always the ones calling the shots. But here's a little secret: Men, too, relish the thrill of being pursued. We want to feel desired, not just like a soldier marching into action!

Surprisingly, the role of the initiator can sometimes be a bit of a turnoff, especially when the partner isn't responding with the enthusiasm of a cheerleader at a championship game. If you find yourself always taking the lead, you might want to reconsider your approach. Remember, sex is a two-way street. If your partner isn't satisfied, it's not just a missed connection but a one-sided performance.

So, my fellow gentlemen, it's time to drop the "I'm in charge" facade. You don't always have to be the commanding officer; sometimes, it's perfectly delightful to embrace your inner playful puppy. Let your guard down, engage in some delightful spontaneity, and discover the joy of mutual exploration. After all, in the grand adventure of intimacy, it's not about who leads the way but how wonderfully you can navigate together!

PERSPECTIVE 5: MEN ARE ALWAYS EXPERIENCED IN SEX

Ah, the age-old myth that men emerge from the womb as seasoned sexual connoisseurs, armed with an arsenal of techniques and boundless confidence. In reality, many men are merely skilled pretenders, donning their bravado like a superhero cape to dodge the dreaded ridicule of being deemed "inexperienced."

Let's be honest: While some men have indeed racked up a colorful portfolio of sexual escapades, others are just starting their journey in the bedroom. And you know what? That's perfectly okay! It's as normal to be a novice as it is to fumble through your first attempts at parallel parking—awkward but totally survivable.

The pressure to be a 'sex guru' can weigh heavily on many men, distorting their self-image and often leading to a performance more theatrical than authentic. So, if you find yourself navigating the uncharted waters of sexual experience, embrace your status as a newcomer! After all, every expert was once an amateur, and the best part of learning is that delightful moment of discovery—like finally figuring out how to fold a fitted sheet.

When you approach your sexual journey with an open mind and a willingness to learn, you invite the opportunity for genuine connection. Communicating openly with your partner(s) not only liberates you from the shackles of expectation but also allows you to explore your desires in a way that feels true to you rather than molded by societal pressures. So, let go of the myth and remember: It's not about the number of positions you can master but about finding joy in the journey of discovery—preferably without any awkward stumbles!

PERSPECTIVE 6: AN ERECTION MEANS SEXUAL AROUSAL

It is a widely held belief that a man's erection is a definitive indicator of sexual arousal. While it is true that men often achieve erections in response to sexual stimuli, this connection is not as straightforward as it may seem. The phenomenon of an erection is influenced by a myriad of biological, psychological, and situational factors that collectively complicate the narrative surrounding male sexual arousal.

At the biological level, erections result from a complex interplay of hormones, nerve signals, and blood flow. When a man is sexually stimulated, the brain releases neurotransmitters that increase blood flow to the penis, resulting in an erection. However, this physiological response can be affected by numerous variables. For instance, elevated stress levels, anxiety about performance, or even fatigue can inhibit this process, leading to situations where a man may feel aroused yet fail to achieve an erection.

Moreover, psychological factors play a pivotal role in sexual arousal. Emotional connections, mental well-being, and contextual influences—such as the dynamics of a relationship or external stressors—can all impact a man's ability to respond physically to sexual stimuli. In some cases, men may experience sexual arousal that does not culminate in an erection due to a variety of cognitive or emotional barriers. This disconnect highlights the importance of understanding that sexual arousal is not merely a physiological response but also deeply intertwined with mental and emotional states.

It is essential to challenge the notion that an erection serves as the sole measure of sexual desire. This reductionist view can lead to misunderstandings and feelings of inadequacy among men, particularly in a society that often equates virility with the ability to maintain an erection. By acknowledging that sexual arousal can manifest in diverse ways, such as desire, fantasies, or emotional intimacy, we can cultivate a more nuanced understanding of male sexuality.

Furthermore, it is critical to promote a narrative that emphasizes open communication about sexual health and experiences. Encouraging men to express their feelings and concerns regarding their sexual function can lead to healthier relationships and greater sexual satisfaction. This also includes recognizing that erections, while important, are not the only markers of sexual health or interest; intimacy and connection can flourish in the absence of an erection.

In conclusion, while erections are a significant aspect of male sexuality, they should not be regarded as the definitive indicator of sexual arousal. Embracing a more holistic understanding of sexual desire—one that incorporates both biological and psychological dimensions—can lead to a healthier discourse around male sexuality, ultimately fostering greater empathy and awareness in both men and their partner(s).

In contemporary society, many men grapple with stigmatization surrounding their sexuality, often feeling ashamed of expressing it authentically. This shame frequently stems from societal expectations that dictate how men should behave sexually. Adherence to a predefined sexual script—a set of cultural guidelines that shape sexual behavior and expression—can be especially restrictive.

To elucidate, consider the concept of a script in performance art. Just as an actor follows a script that directs their movements, dialogue, and mannerisms, individuals navigate sexual scripts that inform their desires, orientations, and behaviors. These scripts are not merely personal; they are influenced by a myriad of external factors including politics, culture, media, and interpersonal relationships. The foundational work of sociologists William Simon and John Gagnon in their 1973 book "Sexual Conduct" introduced the theory of sexual scripts, which posits that our sexual lives are orchestrated by societal norms and expectations.

For example, when a man invites a woman on a date, societal scripts typically dictate that he should cover the cost of the meal. Departing from this expectation can lead to negative consequences, such as disappointing the woman if she subscribes to traditional norms. These learned behaviors are shaped by family, religion, media, and peer influence, demonstrating that sexual scripts are acquired rather than innate.

Understanding that we are all sexual beings—each with unique sexual scripts—allows us to reflect on how these scripts influence our attitudes toward intimacy. Sexual scripts dictate not only how we perceive our partner(s) but also how we engage with our own sexual drives. By examining these scripts, we can begin to recognize their impacts on our sexual lives, revealing how societal norms can restrict our expressions of sexuality.

KEY TAKEAWAYS

Redefining Pleasure: Sexual experiences should prioritize mutual enjoyment and satisfaction between partners, transcending societal pressures.

Individuality in Sexuality: Society often generalizes men's sexual experiences, failing to account for the diversity of individual desires and expressions.

Value of Variety: Quick encounters can be as fulfilling and passionate as prolonged intimacy, emphasizing that quality matters more than duration.

Embracing Spontaneity: Sexual relationships should foster spontaneity and simplicity rather than adhering to rigid expectations.

Breaking Free from Stigma: Many men feel constrained to conform to societal expectations, which can inhibit their authentic expression of sexuality.

CHAPTER 5
SEX

THE UNEXPECTED LESSON

In the bustling corridors of Woolford University's Union Wednesday was the scent of coffee mingled with the excitement of youth. There lived a charming Black man named Jamal. Tall and athletic, with a warm smile that could light up a room, he was the quintessential college heartthrob. His reputation as a ladies' man preceded him; he had a collection of flings that rivaled a Netflix series at times and a Tyler Perry classic at others. Yet, for all his conquests, Jamal felt a nagging emptiness—his sexual escapades often left him wanting more.

As Jamal navigated the lessons that came with campus life, from overnight studying in dorm rooms to attending the Late-Night Library for extracurricular studies on anatomy to wild frat parties, he found himself caught in a cycle of brief encounters. Each rendezvous was filled with laughter, playful banter, and the kind of chemistry that sparked like a live wire. However, when the dust settled and the sheets cooled, he was left unsatisfied, yearning for something deeper—a connection that transcended the physical.

While attending a friend's party one evening, Jamal met Maya. She was a striking woman with cascading curls showing her Puerto Rican roots, deep brown eyes that twinkled with mischief, and a contagious laugh that could draw in anyone. Their conversation flowed effortlessly, peppered with humor and a shared love for late-night taco runs to El Jalisco. The chemistry was palpable, but Jamal was cautious —he had developed a knack for reading the room, and this one felt different.

As the night wore on and their drinks flowed, Jamal and Maya found themselves nestled in a cozy corner of the restaurant without any onlookers, engaged in a thrilling game of questions over tequila. What started as innocent fun quickly escalated, and before they knew it, they began to open up. They were tangled in each other's arms, lost in the moment. Maya's touch was electric, igniting something in Jamal that he hadn't felt before. It was as if the universe had conspired to create this perfect blend of passion and connection.

When they finally made their way back to Maya's place, the atmosphere was charged with anticipation. Jamal's heart raced as they entered her dimly lit bedroom, adorned with fairy lights that danced along the walls, casting a warm glow. They kissed, and suddenly, everything he had experienced before faded into the background. This was different—this was more than just a physical connection. In the recent past, that had been all he'd needed to successfully achieve an erection and then finish the deal.

As their bodies intertwined, Jamal felt a surge of sensations he had never encountered before. It was as if every nerve ending had been awakened, and with each movement, he discovered new depths of pleasure. It originated from within his tailbone region and radiated to various parts of his body uncontrollably. This feeling was different. Jamal's current ride was electric, with impulses of pleasure moving him like a puppet master. This was the first time he was able to let go of his worries and fully appreciate the vibe and connection. Maya was in tune with him, her breaths synchronizing with his, guiding him through uncharted territory. The laughter, the connection—it all combined into a symphony of intimacy.

Something extraordinary happened. In the throes of rhythmic passion, Jamal experienced a series of waves crashing over him, each one more intense than the last. It was as if he had stumbled upon a hidden treasure chest of pleasure, unlocking multiple orgasms that left him reeling. He had always thought that the pinnacle of pleasure was a singular, explosive climax, but this—this was a rollercoaster of ecstasy that left him energized for more yet bewildered.

"Wow," he gasped, pulling her closer as the aftershocks reverberated through him. "I didn't know it could be like that."

Maya chuckled softly as she moved the locks from his forehead to see his chiseled face. "Welcome to the club, J. It's all about that deep connection."

They lay there, basking in the afterglow, exchanging witty banter and heartfelt confessions. In that moment, Jamal realized he had been searching for quality over quantity all along. The laughter, the intimacy, the shared experience—they culminated into the magic ingredient he had been missing.

As the sun began to rise, spilling golden light into the room, Jamal felt a sense of contentment wash over him. He had found what he had been looking for in the most unexpected of places. The journey through college had taught him many lessons, but none as profound as this: True connection could lead to experiences that were not just satisfying but transformative.

From that day forward, Jamal embraced a new philosophy. He still enjoyed the thrill of romance, but he sought deeper connections, savoring every moment like a fine wine. With Maya, he discovered a partner not just in pleasure but in laughter, late-night conversations, and the joy of genuine intimacy—an unexpected lesson that would shape college, post-college, and career life as he got older.

Before we take time to deconstruct all of the things that just happened here, I think it's best to have a crash course on the emissions process and ejaculation so we can better understand what Jamaal experienced when he was in the throes of rhythmic passion.

THE SYMPHONY OF ORGASM

EMISSIONS

The journey toward orgasm can be likened to a grand symphony, beginning with a delicate prelude that sets the stage for intimacy. As desire builds, the body responds with heightened sensitivity and an increased heart rate, much like an orchestra tuning its instruments in anticipation of a performance. The interplay of touch and connection acts as the conductor, guiding the experience through a rising tension that mirrors the crescendo of a musical piece, where every heartbeat and each breath contributes to the mounting urgency.

When the moment of climax arrives, it represents the peak of this symphonic experience—a powerful release of energy marked by involuntary contractions and an overwhelming sense of pleasure. This thrilling finale is followed by a soothing denouement, where participants bask in the afterglow and reflect on their shared connection. Just as an audience might call for an encore, the aftermath of an orgasm invites renewed intimacy, allowing partners to further explore the depths of their bond. In this ongoing symphony of love and desire, each experience is a unique composition celebrating the beauty of human connection.

EJACULATION

Ejaculation, orchestrated by the brain and its intricate hormonal networks, begins with the brain signaling the onset of arousal. This is primarily achieved through the pineal gland, which regulates sleep cycles in addition to tuning in to sexual stimulation. This activation prompts the hypothalamus to release gonadotropin-releasing hormone (GnRH), leading the pituitary gland to produce luteinizing hormone (LH) and follicle-stimulating hormone (FSH). These hormones serve as crucial messengers that urge the testes to prepare for their vital role in reproduction.

The testes, nestled within the scrotum, generate spermatozoa, which undergo a maturation process in the epididymis—akin to a finishing school. Here, the sperm gain motility as they are readied for their upcoming journey. Once prepared, the sperm travel through the vas deferens, which rhythmically contracts to propel them toward the ejaculatory duct, setting the stage for the final release.

As the sperm make their way, the seminal vesicles and prostate gland contribute vital fluids that nourish and enhance sperm motility, while the bulbourethral glands ensure lubrication for a smooth passage. The urethra then acts as the exit route for both urine and semen, culminating in a powerful contraction of the pelvic muscles that results in ejaculation. This moment represents the exhilarating conclusion of a complex biological process in which sperm and seminal fluid are released, showcasing the remarkable choreography of male reproduction.

Here's a revised version with a smoother flow, including the role of the limbic system in orgasms and ejaculation, along with a musical symphony analogy:

THE LIMBIC SYSTEM: THE BRAIN'S ORCHESTRA

Imagine your brain as the conductor of a grand symphony, orchestrating every note and rhythm of your sexual experiences.

At the heart of this symphony lies the limbic system, a powerful ensemble that directs desire, arousal, and fulfillment. The limbic system is a network of structures, including the hypothalamus, amygdala, and hippocampus, each playing a unique role in your emotional and sexual life.

Hypothalamus: The maestro of this orchestra, it regulates hormones like testosterone, setting the stage for sexual arousal and pleasure.

Amygdala: This section interprets emotional cues and sexual motivation, adding depth and intensity to your experiences.

Hippocampus: While known for memory, it enriches your sexual symphony by linking emotions to past experiences.

THE HYPOTHALAMUS: THE RHYTHM OF DESIRE

The hypothalamus is your body's metronome, keeping the rhythm of sexual arousal steady and strong. It triggers the release of hormones, and when attraction strikes, it initiates a cascade of responses that prepare your body for sexual activity.

THE AMYGDALA: HARMONIZING ATTRACTION

As the emotional interpreter, the amygdala decodes what you find attractive. It processes social cues and emotions, ensuring that your sexual motivations are aligned with both your physical and emotional desires.

THE CRESCENDO: ORGASM AND EJACULATION

In the symphony of sex, the climactic crescendos are orgasm and ejaculation. The limbic system, particularly the hypothalamus, coordinates these responses, synchronizing the physical and emotional elements to reach a peak of pleasure. The amygdala and hippocampus contribute by embedding these experiences into your emotional memory, enhancing future encounters.

EMOTIONAL MEMORY: THE ECHO OF EXPERIENCE

After the crescendo, the hippocampus helps retain the emotional and physical echoes of your experiences. Positive memories can amplify future desires, while negative ones might dampen the symphony. This integration of emotion and memory enriches your sexual life.

ENHANCING YOUR SEXUAL SYMPHONY

Understanding the limbic system's role in your sexual symphony allows you to fine-tune your experiences.

Mindfulness and Relaxation: Reducing stress can enhance limbic function, improving your sexual harmony.

Healthy Lifestyle: Exercise and a balanced diet support the hypothalamus and amygdala, boosting libido and performance.

Emotional Connections: Strong emotional bonds enrich your sexual symphony, merging the physical and emotional into a harmonious whole.

By viewing your limbic system as the conductor of a sexual symphony, you gain insight into the intricate interrelations between your brain and body. This understanding not only enhances your experiences but also deepens your connection with your partner(s), creating a fulfilling and harmonious sexual life.

THREE TYPES OF ORGASMS

Embarking on a journey toward the highest form of enlightenment, I detoured from traditional paths to cultivate a closer relationship with God. This exploration led me to meditation, Qi gongs, and the study of diverse spiritual beliefs. Eventually, I found a tribe in Atlanta named Grand Trine, and I learned extensively about sex, sexual energy, and spirituality. Through this journey, I discovered how to harness my energy for prosperity before the bedroom, in the bedroom, and beyond. I have Master Yao and Grand Trine to thank for my better understanding of myself, my faults, and my true power, leading to transmutation. They also taught me about the three levels of orgasm.

1. **Juvenile Orgasm**: This type of orgasm falls below the minimal levels of energy release and offers limited benefits compared to the other two levels. Individuals seeking sex at this level often prioritize quantity over quality, influenced by inadequate

sexual education and religious teachings that hinder understanding of fulfilling sexual experiences.

2. **Adult-Level Orgasm**: This level represents a more organic experience, engaging a larger portion of the body and yielding psychological, emotional, and neurological benefits that extend beyond mere pleasure. Many adults start at this level, yet many others remain stunted, missing out on the development necessary for higher-level orgasms due to societal norms that distort healthy sexual programming.

3. **High-Level Orgasm (HLO):** Characterized by an extended duration, HLO can last from four to twelve minutes, and couples may experience prolonged orgasmic states. In this heightened state, physical contact is not a prerequisite. Rather, it can occur even in the absence of physical touch as partners engage at a higher level of consciousness. The brain chemistry shifts, promoting creativity and energy, while the activity in the left hemisphere decreases. Achieving HLO requires a solid connection with one's partner(s) and alignment of our physical, energetic, and light bodies.

For instance, during Jamaal's session, he experienced a high-level orgasm despite typically hovering around adult-level orgasms. It was evident that enhancing his connection with his partner, along with some random experiences, allowed him to achieve this moment.

Considering this data alongside aligning various bodies (the cellular body, energetic body, and light body), one could facilitate more frequent HLO experiences on their own or when coupled with a partner.

The exploration of orgasm is not merely a biological journey but a profound symphony of emotional, physical, and spiritual interconnectedness. Understanding the different levels of orgasm can empower individuals to seek deeper connections with themselves and their partner(s), enhancing their intimate experiences. By embracing this knowledge and fostering healthy sexual relationships, we can transform our sexual experiences into true masterpieces of intimacy.

KEY TAKEAWAYS

1. **Journey of Orgasm**: The experience of orgasm can be likened to a symphony, with each stage—prelude, crescendo, and finale—contributing to the overall intimacy and pleasure.
2. **Ejaculation Process**: Ejaculation is a complex biological event that involves the brain's hormonal signaling, the maturation of sperm in the testes, and the coordinated contraction of muscles along the reproductive tract, culminating in the release of sperm and seminal fluid.
3. **Juvenile Orgasm**: Characterized by minimal energy release, this level often prioritizes quantity over quality. Individuals at this stage may lack awareness of fulfilling sexual experiences due to inadequate education and restrictive or inhibitive societal norms.
4. **Adult-Level Orgasm**: This type of orgasm engages more of the body and provides psychological, emotional, and neurological benefits. Many individuals start here but may not progress past this level due to a lack of healthy sexual programming and development.
5. **High-Level Orgasm (HLO)**: Marked by extended duration and the ability to achieve orgasm without physical contact, HLO represents a higher state of consciousness. It often results in increased creativity and energy, and it requires a deep connection with one's partner(s).
6. **Role of Hormones**: The journey of ejaculation is initiated by hormonal signals from the brain, showcasing the intricate connection between emotional arousal and physical response.
7. **The Importance of Connection**: Achieving higher levels of orgasm often depends on the emotional and physical connection between partners, emphasizing the need for intimacy and trust in sexual relationships.
8. **Post-Orgasm Afterglow**: The period following orgasm serves as an important time for reflection and reconnection, reinforcing the bond between partners and enhancing future intimate experiences.

9. **Potential for Growth**: Understanding the different levels of orgasms can empower individuals to pursue healthier sexual experiences, fostering growth in both personal and relational aspects of their lives.

10. **Holistic Approach**: Engaging in practices that align the physical, energetic, and light bodies can increase the likelihood of experiencing higher-level orgasms, enriching one's spiritual and sexual journey.

CHAPTER 6
SEX ENERGY

The arcane tradition of Tantra is frequently misconceived, relegated to murmurs of obscure rites or exotic allurements. Yet, fundamentally, Tantra represents an intricate spiritual odyssey—a rich history interwoven with the filaments of consciousness, vitality, and metamorphosis. It beckons us to explore the synthesis of dichotomies and the sanctified interplay between the corporeal and the transcendental.

At the heart of tantric philosophy lies prana, often delineated as a vital force or sex energy. Prana embodies the quintessential life force that permeates the cosmos, animating all sentient beings. It constitutes the quintessence that fuels our yearnings and creativity, the primordial spark catalyzing transformation and healing. Through tantric praxis, the cultivation and direction of this energy facilitates heightened awareness and spiritual enlightenment.

This journey into the depths of prana unveils a profound understanding of existence itself. It is through conscious engagement with this pervasive energy that individuals can transcend mundane limitations and tap into a reservoir of infinite potential. The mastery of prana is not an esoteric pursuit but a fundamental pathway to achieving harmony within oneself and with the universe.

Prana intricately explores the dynamics of masculine and feminine energies not as gender-specific constructs but as universal archetypes inherent within all individuals. Masculine energy, symbolized by Shiva within tantric cosmology, encompasses attributes such as logic, fortitude, and assertiveness. It represents the force of lucidity, structure, and resolute determination. This energy drives the pursuit of knowledge, the establishment of order, and the manifestation of will.

Conversely, feminine energy, epitomized by Shakti, is the quintessence of intuition, empathy, and creativity. It meanders with the currents of emotion, nurturing and sustaining existence. This energy is the wellspring of compassion, the catalyst for innovation, and the nurturer of life itself. It is through the embrace of Shakti that one finds the capacity for profound connection and transformation.

Both energies are indispensable, and their harmonious equilibrium is the cornerstone of personal and spiritual fulfillment. The interplay between these forces is not a mere balancing act but a dynamic synthesis that propels the evolution of consciousness. In recognizing and integrating these energies, individuals can transcend dualistic thinking to realize their fullest potential.

As we embark upon this exploration of the historical tapestry of Tantra, we shall unveil how these ancient doctrines impart timeless sagacity, steering us toward a profound comprehension of our intrinsic nature and the cosmos that envelops us. Delving into the annals of tantric history, we will discover how these teachings have evolved and adapted, offering insights that are as relevant today as they were in antiquity.

Through this scholarly examination, we aim to illuminate the profound wisdom embedded within Tantra, revealing its potential to transform lives and expand the horizons of human understanding. As we journey through time and tradition, let us uncover the enduring legacy of Tantra and its capacity to guide us toward a more enlightened existence.

KUNDALINI

Kundalini is a Sanskrit term that translates to "coiled snake," symbolizing the powerful energy that resides at the base of the spine. It has its roots in ancient Hindu and yogic traditions, where it is considered the primal life force that governs spiritual development and consciousness.

The origin of Kundalini can be traced back to the early Upanishads and Tantric texts, which describe it as a dormant energy coiled three and a half times around the base of the spine. When awakened, it rises through the chakras (or energy centers) along the spinal column, leading to spiritual enlightenment and profound personal transformation.

THE ROLE OF SEX ENERGY

Sex energy is frequently linked to Kundalini, as both are considered vital life forces. In many traditions, sexual energy is seen as a powerful and transformative force that, when harnessed properly, can contribute to spiritual awakening. This energy is not limited to physical expression but can be transmuted into creative and spiritual endeavors.

In the context of Kundalini, sex energy is often viewed as a catalyst for awakening. Practices such as Tantra emphasize the integration of sexual energy with spiritual practice, aiming to harmonize the physical and spiritual realms. By channeling this energy upward through the chakras, practitioners believe they can achieve heightened states of awareness and spiritual enlightenment.

HISTORICAL PERSPECTIVES

Throughout history, various cultures have recognized the significance of sexual energy and its potential for spiritual growth. In ancient India, the Tantric traditions offered detailed practices for awakening and channeling Kundalini. These practices often included meditation, breath control, and sacred rituals designed to balance and elevate energy.

In the West, the interest in Kundalini gained momentum during the 20th century, particularly through the influence of spiritual teachers and the rise of the New Age movement. Figures like Carl Jung explored Kundalini's psychological dimensions, linking them to the process of individuation and personal development.

MODERN VIEWS

Today, Kundalini yoga and meditation techniques are widely practiced around the world. These practices aim to safely awaken and guide the Kundalini energy, promoting physical health, emotional balance, and spiritual insight. Through breathwork, postures, and mantras, individuals seek to harmonize their inner energies and unlock their full potential.

In summary, the interplay between sex energy and Kundalini represents a profound aspect of the human experience, offering insights into the nature of consciousness and the journey toward spiritual awakening. By understanding and harnessing these energies, individuals can embark on a transformative path of self-discovery and enlightenment.

CHAKRAS AND THE HUMAN ENERGY FIELD

In the dynamic interplay of human energy systems, chakras and nadis serve as vital components for understanding our physical, emotional, and spiritual well-being. Chakras, the energy centers aligned along the spine, are pivotal in regulating different facets of our existence. Meanwhile, the nadis, subtle pathways that weave through the body, enable the flow of prana, or life force, to nourish these centers and maintain harmony within.

The seven major chakras each play a unique role:

1. *Root Chakra (Muladhara):* Located at the base of the spine, this chakra grounds us in the physical world, relating to our basic survival instincts and sense of security. It is the foundation upon which the other chakras build, influencing our feelings of stability and trust.
2. *Sacral Chakra (Svadhisthana):* Situated in the lower abdomen, it governs creativity, sexuality, and the flow of emotions. This chakra is the source of our creative energy and desires, encouraging us to embrace change and passion.
3. *Solar Plexus Chakra (Manipura):* Found in the upper abdomen, it is the seat of personal power, confidence, and self-esteem. This chakra fuels our determination and ability to assert ourselves, influencing our sense of purpose and motivation.
4. *Heart Chakra (Anahata):* Located in the center of the chest, this chakra is the bridge between the physical and spiritual realms. It embodies love, compassion, and empathy, fostering deep connections with others and nurturing our capacity for forgiveness.
5. *Throat Chakra (Vishuddha):* Positioned at the throat, it facilitates communication, self-expression, and truth. This chakra empowers us to express our thoughts and feelings clearly and authentically, enhancing our relationships and personal integrity.
6. *Third Eye Chakra (Ajna):* Situated between the eyebrows, it is the center of intuition, insight, and inner wisdom. This chakra opens the mind to deeper understanding, guiding us through dreams and imagination.
7. *Crown Chakra (Sahasrara):* At the top of the head, it connects us to higher consciousness and spiritual enlightenment. It represents our connection to the divine and our understanding of the universe's greater mysteries.

The human energy field, or the aura, extends from these chakras, creating a vibrant halo that interacts with the world and people around us. This field is dynamic, being constantly influenced by our thoughts, emotions, and environments. It acts as a protective shield and a medium for connection, allowing us to resonate with others on an energetic level.

When two individuals come together, their energy fields overlap, facilitating an exchange of energy, emotions, and insights. This interaction can lead to profound empathy, understanding, and even healing. In intimate relationships, especially those involving sexual energy, the lower chakras become activated, and energy can ascend through the central channel, or sushumna nadi, toward the higher chakras.

This rising of energy, often referred to as the awakening of Kundalini, can lead to heightened states of consciousness, spiritual growth, and emotional healing. It transforms physical pleasure into a powerful spiritual experience, fostering a deeper connection with both oneself and one's partner(s).

By understanding and balancing our chakras, we can cultivate a harmonious energy field, enhancing our ability to connect deeply with others and aligning ourselves with the universe's greater flow. This journey of energy alignment not only enriches personal well-being but also strengthens the energetic bonds we share, creating a profound sense of unity and peace.

TANTRIC SEX CENTER (BODY) VS. LIMBIC SYSTEM (BRAIN)

In Tantra, the notion of the sex center being rooted in the body draws fascinating parallels with the limbic system, which plays a crucial role in managing emotions and primal instincts. Both systems underscore the profound connection between our physical sensations and emotional experiences, highlighting their jointly integral roles in shaping human consciousness and behavior.

The limbic system, often dubbed the "emotional brain," is central to processing emotions, memories, and arousal. It governs our instinctual drives, such as the fight-or-flight response, and plays a pivotal role in forming emotional bonds. Similarly, the tantric understanding of the sex center views it as a reservoir of potent energy that can be cultivated and directed for both personal and spiritual transformation.

In the practice of Tantra, engaging the sex center with awareness and intention can lead to heightened states of consciousness. This mirrors how cultivating an understanding of our emotional responses through the limbic system can enhance emotional intelligence and bring about greater psychological resilience. Tantra teaches that by consciously focusing on the body's energy centers, individuals can unlock deeper levels of awareness and connection both within themselves and with others.

The integration of these energies involves practices such as breathwork, meditation, and mindful movement, all of which help channel sexual energy toward spiritual awakening. This holistic approach encourages harmony between the mind, body, and spirit, using the energies of desire and emotion as pathways to enlightenment.

By exploring the tantric sex center's parallels with the limbic system, we gain insights into the deeply interconnected nature of our physical and emotional selves. Both systems remind us of the power that lies in embracing our primal energies and emotions, transforming them into tools for personal growth and spiritual evolution. In this way, Tantra offers a pathway to transcendence that is rooted in the profound wisdom of the body and its innate energies.

Chapter 3 provides a rich exploration of the intricate connections between sex energy, Kundalini, and the broader principles of Tantra. It emphasizes that Tantra is not merely a set of exotic practices but a profound spiritual journey that invites individuals to engage with the vital force of prana, allowing for personal transformation and enlightenment. The chapter highlights the duality of masculine and feminine energies as essential to achieving harmony and balance within oneself, transcending traditional gender constructs. Additionally, the awakening of Kundalini through the harnessing of sexual energy is depicted as a powerful catalyst for spiritual growth, promoting a deeper understanding of consciousness and existence. By integrating these insights into our lives, we can navigate our spiritual odyssey with clarity and intention, fostering an understanding of ourselves and our interconnectedness with all life.

KEY TAKEAWAYS

1. **Understanding Prana**: Prana, or vital force, is the essence of life that fuels creativity, transformation, and healing.
2. **Masculine and Feminine Energies**: These energies are universal archetypes that exist within everyone, representing logic and intuition, respectively. Recommendation: Purchase Awakening the Mater Masculine by Master Yao Nyamekye Morris and his teachings on the House of Man. This details a higher understanding of the four archetypes of men, as we have both masculine and feminine energy.
3. **Kundalini Awakening**: The awakening of Kundalini through sexual energy can lead to profound spiritual insights and personal transformation.
4. **Chakra Balance**: Proper alignment and balancing of the chakras promote overall well-being and facilitate the flow of prana.
5. **Energetic Connections**: The human energy field allows for deep connections with others, enhancing empathy and understanding.
6. **Transformative Relationships**: Intimate connections, especially those involving sexual energy, can elevate experiences to spiritual dimensions.
7. **Holistic Healing**: Engaging with these energies supports emotional healing and personal growth.
8. **Integration of Teachings**: Embracing the principles of Tantra provides pathways toward greater self-discovery and unity with the cosmos.

CHAPTER 7
WHAT IS PLEASURE?

P leasure, in its most profound form, is the essence that drives us toward connection and intimacy. For men, understanding pleasure as a motivating factor for healthy sex begins with an exploration of anticipation—a powerful tool that enhances desire and deepens the sexual experience.

Anticipation is about more than just waiting; it's about cultivating a sense of curiosity and excitement that ignites desire long before any physical touch occurs. It invites you to engage with your partner(s) on multiple levels, exploring the nuances of attraction and the subtleties of connection. This process not only amplifies the eventual physical encounter but also enriches the emotional and psychological dimensions of intimacy.

By taking the time to build anticipation, you create a space for discovery and exploration. It becomes an opportunity to communicate and understand each other's desires and boundaries, fostering a deeper emotional bond. This journey encourages you to be present, to savor each moment, and to engage fully with your partner(s), transforming fleeting interactions into more meaningful encounters.

Moreover, anticipation enhances the overall experience by allowing desire to build gradually, intensifying the pleasure when it finally unfolds. This deliberate pacing leads to a more satisfying and holistic experience, where the focus shifts from merely achieving an end goal to enjoying the process itself.

In embracing anticipation, you unlock the potential for a more authentic connection that nurtures both physical and emotional intimacy. This approach not only enhances sexual health but also contributes to a more fulfilling relationship, where pleasure is not just an act but a shared journey of discovery and delight.

ACCESSING SEXUAL PLEASURE

While sex can be incredibly pleasurable, not all men experience a fulfilling sex life. Several factors might contribute to this lack of satisfaction.

One common issue is engaging in sex without feeling genuinely aroused. Sexual arousal is driven by hormones, and without their release, enjoyment may be compromised. Additionally, participating in sex when not mentally or emotionally prepared can lead to dissatisfaction. Concerns about body image can also impact pleasure, as stress and self-consciousness about appearance can lower libido.

Past negative sexual experiences may also hinder present enjoyment, as dwelling on these memories can impede arousal and satisfaction. Moreover, certain medications, such as diuretics, blood pressure drugs, and mood stabilizers, may affect libido and hormone release, thus impacting pleasure. Certain medical conditions may also cause uncomfortable sexual experiences. It's crucial to discuss these issues with a healthcare provider who can offer adjustments or referrals to specialists to ease the process of improvement.

Despite these challenges, it's possible to enjoy a fulfilling sex life by consciously deciding to enhance your experience. Effort and patience are key, as sexual satisfaction evolves over time. Embrace the natural ebb and flow of your sexual journey. Sex isn't always easy, but navigating changes can lead to growth and deeper enjoyment. Treat these changes as valuable learning experiences rather than setbacks, and focus on maximizing pleasure even during challenging times.

Here are some strategies to help you explore and enhance sexual satisfaction with your partner(s):

HAVE THE SEX TALK

Before diving into the sheets, let's chat! Start with the thrilling tale of your daily escapades, because who doesn't want to know how your coffee run relates to your libido? Discuss consent like it's the latest Netflix series everyone's raving about, and throw in some safety tips like you're giving out life hacks.

Let's talk about that morning wood! It's like your body's way of saying, "Surprise! Time to rise and shine!" Share your feelings as they bubble up like a fizzy soda during sweet nothings, because we all know that one ear gets you going more than the other.

Then there's the classic debate over positions—let's make it less of a wrestling match and more of a strategic game of Tetris. Flexibility? Check. Angles? Double check. You want to impress your partner(s), not make them feel like they're in a yoga class!

EAT HEALTHY FOOD

Now, I know what you're thinking: "How can kale possibly make my sex life sizzle?" Well, trust me, a balanced diet can do wonders! Think of it as fueling your sexual engine—healthy food is like premium gas for your libido. Plus, it helps produce those hormones that turn up the heat in the bedroom.

ABSTAIN A BIT

Want to spice things up? Try a little abstinence! It's like going on a diet before the big feast—trust me, you'll miss it so much that you just might start daydreaming about it. Anticipation is key; it's the best appetizer for the main course!

PUT SEX IN YOUR SCHEDULE

Yes, you heard that right—schedule it! It may sound as romantic as a dentist's appointment, but trust me, knowing you've got some sexy time on the horizon can keep you on your toes. It's like planning a mini-vacation, but with less sunscreen and more…well, you know.

SPICE THINGS UP

If your sex life is starting to resemble a stale loaf of bread, it's time to knead it! Get creative—experiment with new positions, toys, or even a new playlist. Let's bring some flavor back into the mix!

RELAX

Remember, sex should feel like a cozy blanket, not a high-pressure situation. After a long day, unwind with some romantic tunes or binge-watching your favorite show. A relaxed mind equals a happy body—so make sure to chill before you thrill!

EXERCISE

Let's be real: A little exercise goes a long way! Not only does it boost your stamina, but it also gives you that confidence boost that'll have you strutting into the bedroom like you own the place. So, hit the gym. Your future self (and partner[s]) will thank you!

LET GO OF THE PAST

This was my personal issue as it relates to relationships in general and sexual experiences. Not letting go took a toll on how I made love. If past experiences have you feeling like a deer in the headlights, it might be time to seek professional help. You deserve to enjoy sex without the ghosts of relationships past haunting your fun!

APPLY LUBRICANTS

Even the best of us need a little extra help sometimes—cue the lubricants! Think of them as the cherry on top of your sundae; they make everything smoother and way more enjoyable.

FOREPLAY

Don't rush the good stuff! Foreplay is like the warm-up act before the main performance, so give it the time it deserves. Those tender moments build anticipation and turn up the excitement dial!

SEE A DOCTOR

If you've tried all the tricks in the book and nothing's working, it's time to consult a medical professional. Sometimes your body needs a little help from a friend—in this case, a doctor!

MEDITATE/QI GONG

Lastly, consider meditation or Qi Gong. It's like yoga for your sexual response, lowering cortisol (stress) levels and boosting your mood. Who knew that finding your Zen could lead to better sex?

BUILD A RELATIONSHIP WITH YOUR PENIS

And finally, let's talk about building a solid relationship with your most trusted sidekick. Get to know him—what makes him tick? Does he respond better to more lube? The more you know, the better your adventures will be!

CHAPTER 8
SEX AND MUSHROOMS

MUSHROOMS AND THE MIND-BODY CONNECTION IN SEX

My first experience with shrooms began with my tribe. We participated in a spiritual plant-based ritual that I had no idea would bring the enlightenment, awareness, and calmness that I needed at the time. I was going through a difficult breakup which had caused a financial strain. My basic needs were impacted, and the only people I knew to love and trust were my parents and sister. Anybody else was one mistake away from getting their asses handed to them, but at least it was going to be on a silver platter.

The day came for me to embark on a new spiritual journey with the unsuspecting spiritual results being orgasms of power. The tribe started by dressing in white, which isn't different from typical rituals. Plus, I was around people I had started to form new relationships with over the past two months. I was in control. I was good—or so I thought. Something about this ritual was unlike any other. I had been a part of rituals with fraternities, honor societies, and community programs, but none had carried the energy I felt in the room. Those ceremonies felt plastic in nature. Not real. This one connected with all of my senses from the time the tribe entered the ceremony room.

We all got in formation to ingest the shrooms. Honey, chocolate, and shrooms were measured by the goddess leading the show for each person. She spoke to spirit, giving her the answers needed to supply us with just enough to have a spiritual experience. It was time for things to get started. The men in the tribe had been holding space for the women, getting them ready to bring the energy into the room that was needed for us to go on this experience—which I still had no idea about. But I listened with my heart, got out of my shell, trusted the process, and allowed the process to take control. The women were escorted into the room with their sensual and sexy outfits on. The men formed around them, looking sharp and holding this energy in a container as the masculine energy. It was showtime. We all ingested the three items given to us. Some had more or less than others, but each person had just enough.

The leader of the show and Tantra Master led this experience, speaking life into the crowd. Slowly but surely, the women started to go into orgasm, further bringing in the spirit and lifting the sex energy in the room. The energy was thick and filled the room until you could cut it with a knife—a spiritual one, at least. I sat with my spiritual brother thinking I must have gotten somebody else's dosage. Boy was I wrong. Just as quickly as doubt set in, the journey began a few ticks before CP time. The leader gave us permission to take our trip as if she were the conductor on this train going to a place we'd never been before. I was off. Instantly, I was out of my head, and all of my worries mattered not.

I was surveying the room and trying to find what I was feeling. All of my senses had a conversation with me at that time. Hearing the moans of women in orgasmic bliss got me all kinds of excited. Seeing the white around with my eyes open and now closed left images of angels floating around the room. Were they here to usher me to another place? The place smelled of sweet honey and chocolate, and it was good. It tasted good, too. Then I was feeling on myself, trying to gain answers to life. I had a million questions going on in my head. And boom. An orgasm? How? I lifted off, closed my eyes, and let the journey take me to a place I'd never been before. Was this heaven? Where was I? It felt so fucking good. I was now in a space where there was nothing but me and images of whiteness...stillness. I continued to have orgasms and could feel tears rolling down my eyes while they were shut. My consciousness was now reaching out in search of God. This had to be heaven. As I was searching for God's face, God's voice, God's presence, the thing I could hear, see, and feel was myself. In search of something external, I began to understand all that I needed was within. The tears continued to flow. I began to experience a strong connection with those around me. From that point forward, this was my tribe, my family. We had a connection with the higher, together as one.

In the exploration of sex and spirituality, psychedelic mushrooms and their profound impact on our sensual experience offer a rich avenue for understanding the mind-body connection. This chapter delves into how these natural substances can enhance our awareness, deepen intimacy, and foster a greater sense of connection with ourselves and our partner(s). By examining the historical, spiritual, and practical aspects of using psychedelic mushrooms, we create a holistic understanding of their role in enhancing sexual experiences.

PSYCHEDELIC MUSHROOMS AND THEIR EFFECTS ON SENSUALITY AND SPIRITUALITY

Psychedelic mushrooms, particularly those containing psilocybin, have been utilized for centuries across various cultures as sacred tools for spiritual awakening and self-discovery. From the indigenous Mazatec people of Mexico to contemporary psychonauts, the use of these mushrooms has often been associated with rituals aimed at expanding consciousness and connecting with the divine.

When consumed, these mushrooms can drastically alter perception, heighten sensory experiences, and foster a profound sense of unity with the universe. Many users report an enhanced appreciation for touch, taste, and visual stimuli, transforming ordinary sexual encounters into experiences of profound ecstasy and connection.

This heightened state of sensuality allows individuals to explore their own and their partners' bodies with a refreshed sense of curiosity and reverence. Rather than approaching sex as a mechanical act, the use of psychedelic mushrooms can encourage a more holistic understanding where every touch feels amplified, every kiss is deepened, and intimacy transcends the physical. Users often describe encounters that feel transcendent, as if they are not just engaging in a physical act but in a cosmic dance of energies.

Moreover, the spiritual dimensions of these experiences can lead to a deeper emotional bond between partners. Engaging in sexual intimacy under the influence of psilocybin can illuminate personal insights and shared vulnerabilities, allowing couples to navigate complex emotional landscapes together. This can foster a sense of safety and trust, where partners feel empowered to express their desires and boundaries more openly. Ultimately, such experiences can lead to a more profound understanding of one's sexuality as a spiritual practice—an exploration of the divine within the self and in the other.

MIND-ALTERING PROPERTIES AND THEIR INFLUENCE ON SEX

The mind-altering properties of psychedelic mushrooms can significantly influence sexual experiences by promoting an enhanced state of mindfulness and presence. In a world filled with distractions and societal pressures, the effects of psilocybin can create a serene mental landscape that encourages individuals to focus on the present moment. This state of flow allows the mind to quiet, enabling the body to take the lead in a more instinctual and primal way.

During intimate moments, this heightened presence can facilitate deeper connections between partners, allowing for a level of communication that transcends words. Many individuals find that, under the influence of psychedelics, they become more attuned to their partner's needs and desires. This can lead to an increased ability to read non-verbal cues and foster a richer, more empathetic intimacy.

Additionally, psychedelic experiences often encourage introspection, helping individuals confront personal issues related to sexuality like shame, guilt, and anxiety. Many people carry emotional baggage that can hinder their sexual enjoyment and connection with their partner(s). Through the lens of psychedelics, these issues can be surfaced in a safe and supportive environment, offering individuals a chance to work through them. By addressing these emotional barriers, individuals can emerge with a more liberated approach to their sexual selves, embracing their desires and identities more fully.

This transformative process can also inspire creative expression, enabling partners to explore new dimensions of intimacy. Whether through dance, art, or verbal expression, the creative flow often unlocked by psilocybin can enhance the sexual experience, allowing for a playful exploration of each other's bodies and desires. This creativity can lead to a sense of liberation that enriches both the sexual act and the overall relationship.

CONSIDERATIONS FOR SAFE AND MINDFUL MUSHROOM USE

While the potential benefits of psychedelic mushrooms in enhancing sexual experiences are intriguing, it is essential to approach their use with caution and respect. Mindful preparation is key. Before embarking on this journey, consider the following guidelines:

1. **Set and Setting**: Ensure you are in a safe, comfortable environment. The surroundings should be free from distractions and potential interruptions, as the environment can significantly impact your experience.
2. **Open Communication**: Prior to using mushrooms, have an honest conversation with your partner(s) about intentions, boundaries, and comfort levels. Discuss what you hope to achieve and any concerns. Establishing a safe word can be a helpful way to maintain comfort throughout the experience.
3. **Dosage**: Start with a lower dose to gauge your sensitivity and reaction. Everyone's body responds differently, and starting low can both minimize anxiety and enhance the experience.
4. **Mindfulness Practices**: Engage in mindfulness exercises such as deep breathing, meditation, or yoga before consumption. These practices can help ground you and set a positive intention for the experience.

5. **Legality of Psilocybin Mushrooms**: The legal status of psilocybin mushrooms varies widely across different jurisdictions. In some areas, they are classified as illegal substances, while others have decriminalized or legalized their use for therapeutic and/or recreational purposes. It is crucial to research and understand the laws in your region before considering their use.

6. **Possession and Distribution**: Possessing or distributing psilocybin mushrooms can lead to legal repercussions, including fines and imprisonment. Engaging in communal experiences or sharing mushrooms may carry additional legal risks, so be aware of the implications of your actions.

7. **Health Risks and Medical Conditions**: Individuals with a history of mental health issues, particularly those related to psychosis or severe anxiety, should be cautious when considering psychedelics. Psilocybin can exacerbate certain conditions, leading to potentially harmful outcomes. Consulting with a healthcare professional before use is advisable.

8. **Quality Control and Sourcing**: The potency and purity of psychedelic mushrooms can vary significantly. Sourcing from reputable suppliers is essential to minimize the risk of consuming contaminated or misidentified substances. Researching the source and ensuring the proper identification of mushroom species is critical.

9. **Informed Consent and Shared Experiences**: When engaging in psychedelic experiences with a partner, both individuals should provide informed consent beforehand. This means understanding the potential risks and benefits, as well as being aware of how the experience may affect each partner differently.

10. **Aftercare and Integration**: Following the experience, it is beneficial to engage in aftercare to process the insights gained and address any challenging emotions that may have arisen. Integration therapy, whether through individual reflection or

professional guidance, can help solidify the lessons learned and support ongoing personal growth.

KEY TAKEAWAYS

- **Psychedelic mushrooms can enhance intimacy and connection** through heightened sensory perception and emotional bonding.
- **Historical use** spans various cultures, often linked to spiritual practices and self-discovery.
- **Mindfulness and presence** foster deeper connections and improve non-verbal communication between partners.
- **Emotional barriers** related to sexuality can surface, providing an opportunity for healing and liberation.
- **Creative expression** during the experience can enrich intimacy and various relationship dynamics.
- **Legal implications** vary by jurisdiction; understanding local laws is crucial before using psilocybin mushrooms.
- **Possession and distribution of psilocybin** can lead to legal consequences, including fines and imprisonment.
- **Health risks exist,** especially for individuals with pre-existing mental health conditions; consulting a healthcare professional is recommended.
- **Quality control** is essential when sourcing mushrooms to ensure safety and potency.
- **Informed consent** is necessary for shared experiences; partners should understand the potential effects.
- **Aftercare and integration** support the processing of experiences and personal growth post-use.

CHAPTER 9
CANNABIS AND SEX

When it comes to the issue of cannabis (marijuana) and sex, there are a lot of mixed reactions. While some folks condemn the plant and do not wish to talk about it publicly, others have been able to identify the benefits related to its consumption in the appropriate dosage. Cannabis is purported to help mitigate anxiety and pain; it makes sense that the substance may also enhance sex indirectly. In addition, several speculations claim that the substance possesses a nearly mythical libido-boosting power. We know what we like to get from the plant in terms of the pleasure experience, but somehow we left the topic out of the main conversations. The question is: Why? The healing powers of the flower cannot be overemphasized, but conversations about the pleasure cannabis brings can be daunting. Maybe you've heard at any time that it is capable of reducing sperm count or leading to erectile dysfunction and even premature ejaculation. Medical cannabis expert at InhaleMD in Boston, Jordan Tishler, M.D., told SELF that when it comes to understanding cannabis and sexuality, more emphasis should be placed on sexuality itself rather than the substance. Dr. Tishler added that researchers might take different aspects into account when examining sexual enjoyment, including social, psychological, and biological factors that possibly contribute to orgasm, arousal, attraction, and overall satisfaction.

UNEXPECTED CANNABIS EFFECTS ON SEX

According to cross-sectional research published in Sexual Medicine, endocannabinoids play a crucial role in sexual functions, with cannabinoid receptors mapped to diverse brain areas involved in sexual function. In addition, both cannabinoids and endocannabinoids interact with hormones and neurotransmitters that mediate sexual behavior. A survey revealed that cannabis could enhance the quality, longevity, and frequency of sexual pleasure, whether you're riding solo or partnered up. Several recent scientific studies have also revealed that cannabis can enhance bedroom activities for both men and women. The makers of the world's first smart vibrator, Lioness, partnered with cannabis delivery service Eaze to further expound on how flower can affect people's sex lives. The report states that irrespective of who you are, cannabis can boost your orgasms. Although a satisfying sex life is dependent on several variables, cannabis can increase the quality, length, and frequency of orgasms and pleasure sessions whether you are married or single, with a partner or alone, or a silver fox or young adult.

Lioness shared the results of the report with their 432 newsletter subscribers in North America between June 23 and July 1. The study included the viewpoint of 19 Lioness users and their experiences after experimenting with different products of cannabis. Products included THC- and CBD-infused vaporizers, lubricants, and edibles. Head of Data Research at Eaze, Peter Gigante, stated in an email that, as cannabis becomes more and more a part of our daily lives, we hope that consumers will be able to realize the various benefits of these substances in the bedroom from the reports presented and encourage people to explore it in the best way possible.

Here are the different ways cannabis can make sex better, according to the report:

LONGER SESSIONS

Participants reported that sex without marijuana consumption lasted 34.6 minutes with a partner, 19.2 minutes independently, and 12.6 minutes with the Lioness smart vibrator. However, when they consumed, 73 percent said their partnered sessions went longer, while 64 percent reported spending more time pleasuring themselves. Married couples were more likely to spend more time enjoying one another while consuming cannabis than single people. The product that participants reported as having "the most significant impact on orgasm length and frequency" was THC edibles.

MORE ORGASMS

Nearly half of the participants said they experienced more orgasms when they consumed marijuana, whether during masturbation or partnered sex (43 percent and 48 percent, respectively). In addition, THC edibles were once again associated with an increase in orgasms.

EASIER TO REACH ORGASM

Sixty-three percent of participants said cannabis made reaching orgasm easier when they were solo, while 71 percent reported the same when with a partner. The report also states that participants could shorten the time to achieve orgasm while solo or with a partner after taking cannabis. The empirical and anecdotal evidence indicated that cannabis could help respondents shorten the time between the commencement of the session and the orgasm.

Lioness data found that the duration of each orgasm itself increased by 14% to 46% and was associated with greater self-reported masturbation satisfaction, according to reports. To back up claims, the average orgasm in the study lasted for 33.6 seconds with cannabis.

MORE SATISFACTION

Eight-five percent and 79 percent of respondents said cannabis helped them feel more satisfied with the quality of their orgasms during solo and partnered sessions, respectively. Using sex toys while consuming cannabis also became more pleasurable for most participants, whether they used them independently or with a partner. That includes 87 percent of married people. Researchers also took a closer look at how THC and CBD impact sex. According to the report's findings, both cannabinoids enhanced the sexual experience. CBD products, however, helped participants reach orgasms "easier," while THC products led to more "intense and satisfying" sessions. In a statement emailed to Marijuana Moment, Lioness co-founder and CEO Liz Klinger talked about the importance of normalizing such conversations around sexual health and pleasure. "For far too long, the benefits of sexual pleasure and cannabis have been overlooked and underfunded due to taboo and fear," she said. "The goal of this report is to continue to drive conversation and education about the effects of cannabis use in the bedroom, and we're excited to share some of the unique findings for both solo and partner sessions."

SEXUAL FREQUENCY

Researchers investigated the relationship between cannabis use and sexual frequency in a population-based study published in the Journal of Sexual Medicine. After adjustment for covariates, the research showed that male marijuana users had more monthly and daily sex than those who never used it. In addition, they observed a trend that revealed that the consumption of cannabis in excess was linked to increased coital frequency. They concluded that the use of cannabis is independently associated with increased sexual frequency and seems not to result in sexual dysfunction. Furthermore, cannabis is likely to slow down the perception of time and elongate pleasurable feelings. It may also reduce sexual inhibitions while boosting confidence and a willingness to experiment. Cannabis is also known to elevate sensations such as sight, touch, taste, smell, and hearing.

THINGS YOU NEED TO KNOW BEFORE YOU MIX CANNABIS AND SEX

Different folks react differently to cannabis since it is a psychoactive drug. If you are trying the plant for the first time, you need to take it in a minute quantity and go at a slow pace. It would be best to take precautions to ensure that you have the most enjoyable and safe experience. In the U.S., cannabis has been legalized for medical use in 33 states plus the District of Columbia, and it is legal for adult (recreational) use in 10 states plus D.C. However, there are age restrictions within those states. As a reminder, it is still illegal at the federal level, meaning there are some obvious legal risks associated with cannabis in the U.S. It is better to try cannabis on your own before incorporating a partner, Dr. Tishler suggested. He added that he usually advises people who wish to use cannabis for sex for the first time to try it out initially with a masturbation event. He speculated that it would enable you to know how you react to cannabis and its effect on your level of arousal and orgasm before embracing a partner and all their variables.

On the contrary, Dr. Lynn says it isn't bad to try it for the first time with a partner you trust in case you freak out. She said that if that happens or you're scared it may happen, having a close partner could be great to help you calm down. No matter what, you should be able to control yourself even though you're using cannabis with another person specifically to enhance sex; the same consent rules apply.

Concerning consent, when you decide to use the substance to enhance your sexual experience with someone else, seek affirmative consent for whatever you intend to do and set your boundaries beforehand. Whether or not you use cannabis, consent is important to ensure everyone is on the same page, so you need to discuss this with your partner(s) ahead of time to ensure you do not trespass. Another important thing to consider is to differentiate whether you want cannabis to give you an enjoyable sexual experience or help you manage a diagnosable sexual dysfunction, the effectiveness of which is yet to be confirmed through research. Finally, of course, cannabis isn't a cure-all, and it can't fix many of the root causes of sexual dysfunction or relationship problems. You may make moves to see a doctor or sex therapist if you are having any symptoms of sexual dysfunction.

Another thing to consider with the use of cannabis for sex is keeping water and lube on hand. There's nothing sexy about cottonmouth or vaginal dryness when trying to get your freak on! Keeping water and lube on hand is important to stay hydrated.

PRECAUTIONS CONCERNING THE OVERUSE OF CANNABIS; EFFECT ON SEXUAL FUNCTION IN MEN

We would like to remind you that the moderate use of cannabis (marijuana) does not result in erectile dysfunction (ED). Still, some researchers have suggested that an association exists between ED and the excessive use of cannabis. The most frequent male sexual disorder is ED, and male infertility is not traced to the use of cannabis.

In addition, cannabis can increase the heart rate and lead to anxiety in some cases. Hence, the overuse or abuse of the plant is detrimental to your health. Finally, it is important to remember that cannabis has the potential for unpleasant side effects, just like all drugs. Cannabis can affect the lungs and aggravate conditions such as asthma, particularly when the substance is smoked.

The American Journal of Men's Health published a systematic review that included five case-control studies with 3,395 healthy men (1,035 cannabis users). The overall frequency of ED was 69.1% vs. 34.7% in the control group. In addition, the odds ratio of ED in cannabis users was close to four times that of the control. In other words, the rate of ED in men who consumed the drug was about twice that of those who abstained from the plant. According to the authors, the link between ED and cannabis consumption is probably a mix of organic and psychological factors. They further said that the mechanisms are likely to result from the endocannabinoid system through the binding of receptors in the paraventricular nucleus region of the hypothalamus, which regulates the erectile function and sexual behavior of males. This mechanism also elucidates why cannabis can enhance sexual function in some patients who are presenting with symptoms or affected by conditions such as pain, depression, and anxiety disorder. Furthermore, ongoing studies, both in animals and humans, have reported a peripheral effect of cannabis on ED, specifically on the corpus cavernosum (two columns of spongy tissue that run through the shaft of the penis) where cannabinoid receptors are present.

THE BEST CANNABIS STRAINS FOR DIFFERENT TYPES OF SEX AND SENSATION

Cannabis can help you take your sexual pleasure to another level, although researchers are still trying to investigate the benefits of cannabis in and out of the bedroom. A study confirmed that 68.5 percent of people said they had more pleasurable sex while using cannabis. Out of curiosity, the cannabis expert and co-founder of GoLove CBD Naturals, John Renko, and the medical cannabis therapeutics specialist and Harvard physician who oversees InhaleMD, Jordan Tishler, were summoned. They gave insights regarding choosing the right strain and product for the most mind-blowing sexual experience irrespective of your mood.

Let's dive into the strains you might consider for different types of sensation and sex. First, the experts argued over the role strains play in terms of their effects. Dr. Tishler feels strains lead to different preferences during sex but don't guarantee any outcomes.

IF YOU WANT TO BOOST YOUR LIBIDO

Renko proposed that it is better to select strains with high levels of the terpene limonene if you wish to intensify your sex drive. Examples are Wedding Cake and Dosidos. These two are indica-dominant, high-THC hybrids that enhance your mood quickly with a body-warming euphoria before it fades out to ecstatic relaxation.

IF YOU'RE SOLO AND ENJOYING SOME ALONE TIME... BETWEEN THE SHEETS

Renko says that if you wish to enhance your drive during a solo session, the best strain is one containing the terpene linalool, which is well known for its nice, calming effect. A good example of popular strains that will help you derive some awesome self-pleasure in a full afternoon is L.A. Confidential, an indica, and Amnesia Haze, a sativa. From users' reports, they experience a slow start before an intense euphoria with a gradual come down.

IF YOU'RE PRONE TO ANXIETY

Cannabis does wonders in this area. Along with anecdotal evidence, current research reveals that cannabis may reduce anxiety. A superficial study conducted in 2018 analyzed the cannabinoids and terpene levels of different strains and identified the most effective ones for treating anxiety. So, if any self-consciousness is disturbing you from having an enjoyable sexual time, you could get your "kush" on.

The top strains for anxiety were:

- Blueberry Lamsbread, a sativa-dominant hybrid
- Kosher Kush, an indica
- Skywalker OG Kush, an indica-dominant hybrid
- Bubba Kush, an indica

IF YOU'RE WORRIED ABOUT POTENTIAL PAIN

Past studies have revealed that not only does cannabis mitigate pain but also that indicas appear to be the preference that could provide pain relief. According to Renko, if you experience pain during sex, you can use strains with terpenes that might relieve you of that pain, such as myrcene, caryophyllene, beta-caryophyllene, and humulene. He believes the best is the strain Zkittlez, an indica-dominant hybrid with a strong beta-caryophyllene and humulene profile.

Other strains to try are:

- Harlequin, a sativa-dominant strain
- G13, a potent indica
- Cannatonic, a low-THC, high-CBD hybrid

IF YOU WANT TO TRY SOMETHING NEW

If you are tired of your usual normal and wish to explore new things sexually, there's anecdotal evidence that some strains can give you that feeling that you crave.

Based on reviews from online users, these strains lower your inhibitions and boost your confidence:

- Atomic Northern Lights, an indica-dominant hybrid
- Blue Dream, a sativa-dominant hybrid
- Granddaddy Purple, an indica
- Trainwreck, a potent sativa-dominant hybrid

IF YOU WANT SOMETHING HIGH-ENERGY

With the right dosage, some strains can provide you with the energy you need to take complete charge in bed.

Based on reviews from online users, these are the strains to consider if you're in the mood for an Energizer Bunny-Esque romp:

- Super Lemon Haze, a zesty sativa
- Green Crack, a sativa
- Cheese Quake, a hybrid

IF YOU WANT SOMETHING RELAXING

If you consume cannabis excessively, you'll surely chill out, so the right thing to do is choose relaxing strains and use them in the right dosage to ensure you get to the right level of chill.

Some examples of relaxing strains include:

- Animal Cookies, a balanced hybrid
- Master Kush, an indica
- Mr. Nice, a sativa

IF YOU WISH TO ENHANCE YOUR SENSITIVITY TO TOUCH

Several experienced cannabis users speculate that certain strains could help increase sensitivity to touch and improve tactile sensations. However, since we all have different body types, it is not unusual to find that some strains work well for you, but they may not work the same way for your partner(s). Renko recommends that if you've been enjoying cannabis for some time, you can balance out your fave THC-dominant strain with a CBD-dominant strain like ACDC. ACDC is a sativa-dominant strain with 14 percent CBD, less than 1 percent THC, and a good terpene profile in addition to the synergistic effect of CBD and THC.

Some examples of other strains to boost erogenous play and give you the tingles are:

- Bubblegum Kush, an indica-dominant strain
- Sour Diesel, a pungent sativa
- Jillybean, an indica-dominant strain

WHAT ELSE CAN YOU USE TO SPICE UP YOUR SEX SESH?

Loads of things! But since we're talking about cannabis and sex, we would mention a few other cannabis products made with sexy time in mind. First, there are various cannabis-infused sex products, such as lubricants and massage oils containing CBD and THC.

THC or CBD Lube

According to people who have tried THC- and CBD-infused lube, it is a wonderful product. The producers of these lubes claim the product provides several benefits, such as increased arousal and an increasingly powerful orgasm. While there is no evidence to support these claims scientifically, that does not mean the postulated benefits are untrue or that cannabis-infused lube is incapable of boosting your sex life. On the contrary, sufficient lubrication is key to comfortable and enjoyable penetrative sex. Also, it just feels great! If you want to give a THC or CBD lube ago, you have a few to choose from, starting with GoLove CBD Intimate Lubricant.

THC or CBD Anal or Vaginal Suppositories

There is limited clinical research on cannabis suppositories, and you should not have overly high expectations of them as there is no evidence that they are absorbed into the bloodstream via the anus or vagina. Of course, this isn't to say that they don't have other effects that can help you below the belt. Users of CBD and THC suppositories confirm that they're great lubricants that help relieve pain during and after anal or vaginal sex in addition to enhancing sexual pleasure.

THC or CBD Massage Oil

A good, oily rubdown isn't a bad idea. The use of oil could be a great way to make your body feel good physically without the "high" since topicals don't enter the bloodstream. A couple of options are CBD Daily Massage Lotion and Papa & Barkley's Releaf Body Oil.

KEY TAKEAWAYS

- Today's climate has a lot to say about people salivating over profits. One of them is California's 31.4-billion-dollar cannabis industry, a market with a blank check to spend. The wonderful effects of cannabis concerning sexual pleasure are enormous, but sadly, most people do not want to pick it up as a point of discussion.
- Several anecdotal pieces of evidence have proven that cannabis enhances sexual pleasure. In addition, past studies have revealed that cannabis users often have more sex than non-users.
- If you intend to prepare your body for pleasure, you need to understand that cannabis is usually well-tolerated when used as directed. All you need to do is ensure you purchase the flower or product from a reputable, licensed source. Then you can go all the way to explore and have fun.

CHAPTER 10
SODAPOP SEX

P op culture is the collection of ideas, beliefs, actions, objects, and practices that are popular in a society at a given time. It shapes and reflects societal norms, often influencing how individuals perceive themselves and the world around them. Historically, pop culture has both defined and redefined social norms across different times and places worldwide. It is a dynamic force driven by creativity, innovation, and sometimes serendipity, creating frameworks through which society absorbs and reacts to new ideas.

Sodapop sex, a term derived from this cultural landscape, refers to the influence of pop culture, social media, and pornography in shaping contemporary views on sex. These influences can create a trance-like distraction that pulls individuals away from grounded, authentic experiences. Instead of connecting deeply with our bodies and enjoying sex as a natural and fulfilling act, we may find ourselves chasing ideals that have been strategically fed to us.

The pervasive influence of social media and pornography often presents sex in an unrealistic, idealized manner. This can lead to feelings of inadequacy and dissatisfaction, as genuine connection and emotional depth are overshadowed by superficial portrayals. These platforms may distort reality, encouraging individuals to measure their experiences against unattainable standards.

Embracing a more grounded approach to sexuality involves tuning in to our authentic desires and needs. This means fostering open communication with your partner(s), prioritizing consent, and cultivating an environment in which vulnerability and trust can flourish. By doing so, we can redefine intimacy as a holistic experience that nurtures both body and spirit.

Moreover, pop culture can be harnessed as a positive force by promoting narratives that celebrate diverse expressions of sexuality and encourage self-discovery. By engaging with content that aligns with our values and supports healthy relationships, we can shift the cultural dialogue toward more empowering and inclusive perspectives.

Ultimately, the goal is to move away from the mesmerization of Sodapop sex and toward a more conscious and fulfilling experience. By reconnecting with our true selves and embracing the God Consciousness within, we can transform our intimate lives and foster deeper, more meaningful connections. Through this journey, we can collectively use pop culture to right the ship and enjoy sex with the awareness and presence that enrich our lives.

THE MODERN TRANCE: DISTRACTIONS AND DISCONNECTION

We are constantly bombarded by notifications, messages, and the lure of infinite scrolling. This incessant digital engagement can create a trance-like state where our attention is perpetually divided. As we navigate between apps and screens, we become increasingly detached from our physical selves. This detachment leads to a diminished awareness of bodily sensations and needs that are crucial for maintaining a healthy mind-body connection.

Being out of touch with our bodies can have profound consequences. It reduces our ability to experience emotions fully and respond to physical cues, impacting our mental health and relationships. This disconnection can manifest as stress, anxiety, and a lack of fulfillment in personal interactions. Cultivating mindfulness and focusing on the present moment can counteract these effects, allowing us to reconnect with ourselves and others more deeply.

HOW MISEDUCATION CONTRIBUTES TO THE DISCONNECTION

Miseducation around sexuality begins early, with many educational systems failing to provide comprehensive or accurate information. This lack of proper education leaves individuals vulnerable to myths and misconceptions that are often perpetuated by peers or unreliable sources. The result is a skewed perception of sexuality and relationships, where unrealistic expectations take root.

This foundation of misinformation leads to a disconnection from authentic sexual identities and healthy relational dynamics. Without a clear understanding of their own bodies and desires, individuals struggle to form genuine connections. By prioritizing a comprehensive sex education that includes emotional intelligence and consent, we can empower individuals to develop healthier, more informed relationships.

THE ROLE OF SOCIAL MEDIA AND EXTERNAL STIMULI IN SEXUAL HEALTH ISSUES

Social media platforms are rife with curated images and narratives that can significantly distort our understanding of sexuality. The idealized portrayals of bodies and lifestyles create a culture of comparison, often leading to insecurity and dissatisfaction with one's own body image. This constant comparison affects self-esteem and can hinder authentic self-expression.

Moreover, the pervasive nature of explicit content online can lead to desensitization and unrealistic expectations regarding intimacy. In the "Penis Book," Dr. Spitz explains that the dorsal anterior cingulate cortex (DACC) drives frequent porn and social media users to seek increasingly novel images. As this region becomes less responsive, individuals feel compelled to "up the ante," constantly seeking more extreme stimuli to achieve the same level of satisfaction.

This distortion impacts sexual health by fostering misconceptions about what constitutes a normal or healthy sexual experience. To combat these effects, it is crucial to engage critically with media, practice digital literacy, and set personal boundaries that prioritize mental and emotional well-being.

THE LINK BETWEEN DISCONNECTED SEXUALITY AND SEXUAL DYSFUNCTIONS

Disconnected sexuality, driven by digital distractions and misinformation, plays a significant role in the development of sexual dysfunctions. When individuals are detached from their bodies and emotions, they may find it challenging to experience pleasure or engage fully in intimate relationships. This disconnection can result in both physical and emotional barriers during sexual activity, such as reduced libido, performance anxiety, or an inability to achieve satisfaction.

Addressing these dysfunctions involves a holistic approach that emphasizes the importance of mindfulness and emotional connection. By fostering a deeper awareness of one's body and emotions, individuals can overcome these barriers. Techniques such as mindfulness meditation, therapy, and open communication with your partner(s) can lead to more fulfilling and harmonious sexual experiences.

HOW THIS AFFECTS THE BRAIN, SEX, AND YOUR POWER AS MEN

The brain is the central organ governing sexual desire and function, and its chemistry can be significantly altered by digital distractions and external pressures. For men, this disconnection can lead to a diminished sense of sexual power and confidence, impacting relationships and self-esteem. Likewise, the constant barrage of stimuli can alter neural pathways, affecting libido and overall sexual performance.

Reclaiming sexual power involves nurturing a strong mind-body connection. This requires a commitment to self-awareness and prioritizing both mental and physical health. By engaging in activities that promote relaxation and self-reflection, such as exercise, meditation, or journaling, men can enhance their sexual vitality and confidence. This empowerment leads to more satisfying and authentic intimate relationships where individuals feel in control and connected to their desires.

KEY TAKEAWAYS

1. **Mind-Body Connection**: Digital distractions can lead to a disconnect from our bodies, reducing mindfulness and affecting relationships. Prioritizing bodily awareness can enhance well-being and intimacy.
2. **Comprehensive Education**: Miseducation about sexuality fosters disconnection. Emphasizing holistic and accurate sex education can empower individuals to form healthier, more informed relationships.
3. **Critical Media Engagement**: Social media and explicit content often distort perceptions of sexuality. Practicing digital literacy and setting boundaries can mitigate these effects and promote sexual health.
4. **Addressing Sexual Dysfunctions**: Disconnected sexuality can lead to dysfunctions. A holistic approach focusing on mindfulness and emotional connection can help overcome these challenges.
5. **Brain-Body Impact**: Digital stimuli alter brain chemistry, affecting sexual desire and power. Reconnecting with the body through self-awareness and mental health practices can restore vitality.
6. **Empowerment Through Awareness**: Understanding the influence of pop culture, social media, and pornography allows individuals to reclaim control over their sexual health and relationships, leading to a more fulfilled life.

CHAPTER 11
SEX-POSITIVE COMMUNITY

Modern conversations about sex and sexuality are often shrouded in stigma and misinformation, whereas cultivating a sex-positive community presents profound benefits, particularly for straight men navigating their sexual identities. Embracing a sex-positive mindset—defined as being open, tolerant, and progressive toward sex, sexuality, and sexual development—encourages individuals to engage more authentically with their desires and experiences. This openness not only fosters personal growth and self-acceptance but also nurtures healthier relationships with both oneself and others.

When men feel free to express their sexual desires without fear of judgment, they are empowered to explore their identities and preferences in a safe environment. This exploration can lead to deeper self-awareness, allowing them to understand their bodies, desires, and boundaries more clearly. It also creates space for meaningful dialogue about consent, respect, and communication, all of which are essential components of any healthy sexual relationship.

Moreover, a sex-positive community dismantles the traditional stereotypes and toxic narratives often associated with masculinity, encouraging men to embrace vulnerability and emotional honesty, establishing and maintaining a high level of emotional intelligence. By rejecting the notion that sexual prowess is tied to dominance or aggression, men can redefine their relationships, especially sexual relationships, with others and themselves based on mutual respect and genuine connection.

Ultimately, adopting a sex-positive approach enriches not only individual lives but also society as a whole. It fosters a culture of empathy and understanding, where diverse sexual expressions are celebrated rather than stigmatized. By championing a progressive attitude toward sexuality, straight and straight-identifying men, because being straight is also a spectrum of experiences, can contribute to a more inclusive world while paving the way for future generations to embrace their sexual identities with confidence and pride. In this chapter, we will begin a conversation, explore the myriad benefits of becoming sex-positive, and determine how this journey can lead to a more fulfilling and present sexual existence.

The Call for a Sex-Positive Community

In an era where traditional norms around masculinity are being challenged, the call for a sex-positive community is more urgent than ever. Embracing a sex-positive mindset allows straight men to move beyond the confines of outdated stereotypes and engage with their desires in a healthy, affirming way. This shift is not just a personal evolution but a collective movement toward creating a more inclusive society.

Pop culture plays a crucial role in this transformation. From films and television series that portray diverse sexual experiences to music that celebrates empowerment and consent, popular media has the power to shape perceptions and influence attitudes. By normalizing conversations about sexuality and showcasing varied expressions of intimacy, pop culture can help dismantle the stigma surrounding these topics. When men see positive representations of sexual exploration and emotional vulnerability, they are more likely to feel empowered to express their own desires as they seek healthy relationships.

The importance of embracing a sex-positive mindset cannot be overstated. It encourages men to reflect on their beliefs about sex, fostering an environment in which they can openly discuss their experiences without fear of judgment. This mindset promotes self-acceptance and encourages the understanding that sexual development is a natural part of life. It also invites men to challenge harmful narratives that equate masculinity with dominance or emotional detachment, allowing for a more nuanced and compassionate understanding of what it means to be a man.

Fostering a supportive and inclusive community is essential for this transition. By creating spaces where an open dialogue is encouraged, men can share their experiences, learn from one another, and support each other in their journeys toward sexual self-discovery. Such communities can serve as safe havens where vulnerability is celebrated and emotional connections are prioritized. This sense of belonging not only enriches individual lives but also cultivates a culture of empathy and respect, ultimately leading to healthier relationships.

As we move forward, the call for a sex-positive community resonates louder than ever. By embracing this mindset and supporting one another, straight men can contribute to a world where everyone feels empowered to explore their sexuality without fear, shame, or stigma. Together, we can create a more inclusive landscape that honors the diverse experiences of all individuals.

Empowering Men for a Healthy Life

Empowering men to embrace a sex-positive mindset is a crucial step toward fostering a healthier, more fulfilling life. This empowerment begins with acknowledging the responsibility men have in cultivating an environment in which open discussions about sexuality can flourish. By actively choosing to embrace sex positivity, men not only enhance their understanding of desire and intimacy but also set a precedent for those around them. This commitment to openness helps dismantle harmful stereotypes and paves the way for a more compassionate view of sexuality, benefiting both individuals and society as a whole.

Integrating sex positivity into all aspects of life is essential for creating lasting change. It extends beyond the bedroom, influencing how men relate to their partners, friends, and family members. When men approach relationships with a sex-positive attitude, they foster communication and trust, laying the groundwork for deeper emotional connections. This mindset encourages respectful conversations about consent, boundaries, and desires, allowing everyone involved to feel valued and understood.

The ripple effect of embracing sex positivity can be profound, impacting various spheres of life including family dynamics, workplace culture, and even religious communities. In families, men who model healthy attitudes toward sexuality can nurture a safe space for their children to explore and understand their own identities without shame. At work, fostering an inclusive environment that respects diverse expressions of sexuality can enhance collaboration and morale, leading to a more productive atmosphere. Furthermore, within religious contexts, embracing a sex-positive approach can challenge outdated dogmas, encouraging communities to engage in more progressive discussions about love, acceptance, and the human experience.

As men take on the responsibility of promoting sex positivity, they not only enrich their own lives but also contribute to a broader cultural shift. This empowerment fosters healthier relationships and cultivates a society where individuals feel free to express their identities without fear of judgment or stigma. In this journey toward embracing sex positivity, men become agents of change as they create a legacy of understanding and respect that transcends generations.

Key Takeaways

1. Embracing Openness: A sex-positive mindset encourages men to be open and tolerant toward their own desires and the sexual experiences of others, fostering personal growth and self-acceptance.

2. Challenging Stereotypes: By rejecting traditional notions of masculinity tied to dominance and emotional detachment, men can redefine their identities and relationships in healthier, more compassionate ways.

3. Cultural Influence: Pop culture plays a significant role in shaping attitudes toward sexuality; positive representations can help normalize discussions about sex, empowering men to engage more freely.

4. Building Supportive Communities: Creating spaces for open dialogue about sexuality allows men to share experiences and support one another, enhancing emotional connections and reducing stigma.

5. Holistic Integration: Sex positivity should be integrated into all aspects of life, influencing how men relate to their partner(s), friends, family, and colleagues, leading to healthier interactions and relationships.

6. Ripple Effects: Embracing sex positivity impacts various spheres of life, including family dynamics, workplace culture, and religious communities, fostering environments of understanding and respect.

7. Legacy of Change: By taking responsibility for promoting sex positivity, men can contribute to a cultural shift that empowers future generations to explore their sexual identities confidently and without shame.

CHAPTER 12

PRAYER OUTRO

This is a prayer for both man and woman, with a shared prayer while making love. Remember to focus and shift conscious energy while emission is happening before cumming.

INTIMACY PRAYER FOR MANIFESTING PROSPERITY AND PROTECTION

MAN'S PRAYER

"As I connect with my beloved, I call upon the divine energy within me. I breathe in, and my consciousness shifts from my mind to my heart, filling me with love and compassion. I then bring my awareness to my lingam, the symbol of creation and manifestation.

"By the power of our union, I pray for protection and prosperity to surround my woman. May our love be a shield against all harm, a beacon of light in the darkness. May our intimacy ignite a fire of abundance, filling our lives with joy, health, and wealth.

"As I move within you, my love, I envision a vortex of energy swirling around us. This vortex attracts all that is good, all that is pure, and all that is life-affirming. May our love be the magnet that draws in the blessings of the universe.

"I call upon the ancient powers of masculine and feminine energies of creation and manifestation. May my lingam be the instrument of divine will, channeling the cosmic forces of prosperity and protection into our lives.

"As we unite, I pray that our love becomes the foundation upon which we build our lives. May our intimacy be the source of strength, the wellspring of inspiration, and the sanctuary of peace."

WOMAN'S PRAYER

"As I surrender to the pleasure of our union, I feel my consciousness expanding. My mind lets go, and my heart opens, overflowing with love and devotion. I breathe in, and my awareness flows down to my yoni, the sacred portal of creation.

"In this space, I connect with the divine feminine, the goddess energy that resides within me. I feel her power, her wisdom, and her love. I call upon the ancient powers of femininity, the energies of receptivity and nurturing.

"As I receive my partner's love, I pray that my goddess energy awakens, blessing him with protection and divine guidance. May my yoni be the sanctuary of peace, the haven of safety, and the source of inspiration.

"I envision a golden light emanating from my being, enveloping my husband and filling his life with joy, prosperity, and good fortune. May our love be the bridge between the divine and the human, the sacred and the mundane.

"As we unite, I pray that our love becomes the celebration of life, the dance of the divine, and the song of the universe. May our intimacy be the expression of the infinite, the manifestation of the eternal, and the embodiment of the sacred."

SHARED PRAYER

"As we come together in this sacred union, we call upon the divine energies of the universe. May our love be the key that unlocks the doors of prosperity, protection, and happiness. May our intimacy be the catalyst that ignites the flames of passion, creativity, and inspiration.

"We pray that our union becomes the source of strength, the wellspring of joy, and the sanctuary of peace. May our love be the bridge that connects us to the divine, to each other, and to the world around us.

"As we breathe in, we inhale the divine energies of the universe. As we breathe out, we exhale love, compassion, and blessings. May our intimacy be the expression of the infinite, the manifestation of the eternal, and the embodiment of the sacred."

Ase.

Namaste

ABOUT THE AUTHOR

Boris Chestnut has worked in the sexual health space for over seven years and has over 15 years of experience in behavioral health services. He helps his clients explore and connect with the origins of their sexual experiences and teaches them how to shift their sexual mindset to align with their physical, emotional, mental, and spiritual being through the use of Tantra or energy work.

Growing up in an environment filled with religious dogma and cultural caveats, Boris witnessed firsthand the sexual misguidance many individuals experienced due to a lack of knowledge and judgment-free exploration. He learned that many people encounter blockages with sexual energy and intelligence that often go unnoticed until they confront them in their personal lives, especially in romantic relationships.

After attending Florida State University and earning a bachelor's degree in Psychology, followed by a master's degree in Clinical Social Work, Boris began his professional career serving the community and investing in people and healthy energies. This experience allowed him to support individuals from multiple racial backgrounds and intersectionalities. While living in Tallahassee, Florida, he had the opportunity to volunteer with various organizations that supported and advocated for Black-identifying individuals. One particularly impactful experience involved working with a processing and resource group for sex workers. The focus was to provide resources for women lacking basic needs in unsafe spaces. Boris was deeply moved by the sex workers who bravely displayed the full human experience of sex—encompassing sexual freedom, limitations, satisfaction, and trauma. Seeing the positive impact of participation in expertly guided and informed conversations about sexuality and sexual health taught Boris about the benefits of sexual energy and the power of using it for manifestation.

While attending the University of Michigan, Boris was the only Black cisgender man in his program. Although he gained vital tools, techniques, and methods in sex therapy, he also recognized a broader need for inclusive spaces that address the unique challenges faced by men of diverse backgrounds. This realization fueled his passion for cultivating environments where men can redefine masculinity in healthier, non-toxic ways and confront widespread sexual miseducation.

Boris believes that men of all races working in sexual health spaces can reshape the landscape of love, sex, and connection in relationships. As a minority in the sexual health industry, he is committed to reaching as many people as possible, using his expertise to foster healthy narratives and redefine the conversation around masculinity and sexuality.

Boris currently resides in Texas, where he provides virtual and in-person support to individuals, couples, groups, and community endeavors. Connect at www.backtothebasex.com.

www.ingramcontent.com/pod-product-compliance
Lightning Source LLC
Chambersburg PA
CBHW061651120626
46550CB00003B/911